MAKE
YOUR
VOICE
HEARD

SECOND EDITION

An Actor's Guide to Increased Dramatic Range through Vocal Training

Date: 1/27/12

MAKE YOUR VOICE HEARD

SECOND EDITION

An Actor's Guide to Increased Dramatic Range through Vocal Training

CHUCK JONES

With a Foreword by Caymichael Patten
and a Preface by Katie Bull

BACK STAGE BOOKS
An Imprint of Watson-Guptill Publications / New York

*To Josleen Wilson, Ryland Jordan, and David Farkas,
and to the memories of Beatrice A. Jones, Charles S. Jones,
and Roy London*

Acquisitions Editor: Mark Glubke
Project Editor: Alexis Greene / Katherine Happ
Designer: Sivan Earnest
Production Manager: Hector Campbell

First published in 2005 in the United States by Back Stage Books,
an imprint of Watson-Guptill Publications,
a division of VNU Business Media, Inc.,
770 Broadway, New York, NY 10003
www.wgpub.com

Library of Congress Cataloging-in-Publication Data
The CIP data for this title is on file with the Library of Congress
Library of Congress Control Number: 2005929288
ISBN: 0-8230-8370-5

Every effort has been made to trace the ownership of and to obtain permission to repro-
duce the material in this book. The author, editors, and publisher sincerely apologize
for any inadvertent errors and will be happy to correct them in future editions.

Printed in the United States

First Printing, 2005

1 2 3 4 5 6 7 8 / 12 11 10 09 08 07 06 05

ACKNOWLEDGMENTS

I have had the great good fortune to work with some remarkable people, many of whom have made generous contributions to this book.

I want to thank David Wells, Katie Bull, Emily Caigan, Judylee Vivier, Francine Zerfas, Mark Glubke, Adina Porter, Paul Lukas, Dale Ramsey, Nels Hennum, Gloria Hale, Ziva Kwitney, David Farkas, Elizabeth Himelstein, Linda deVries, Tanya Berezin, Edie Falco, Carla Gugino, Jessica Hecht, Thom Jones, Deborah Laufer, Joan Potter, Francie Swift, Lisa Story, and anyone I have failed to mention.

I also owe Joe Stockdale, Howard Stein, Caymichael Patten, David Garfield, Linda Swenson, Michael Howard, and Ryland Jordan a special thanks for many years of support.

I could not have done this book without the exceptional help and guidance of Alexis Greene, who edited this book. Her important input has been extraordinary, and I am so grateful to her.

A NOTE TO MY READERS

The exercises described in this book have been used successfully by thousands of actors. If any exercises cause discomfort, eliminate them from your practice. Please see your physician and get his or her approval on the exercises.

—CHUCK JONES

CONTENTS

FOREWORD

BY CAYMICHAEL PATTEN

Director, the Caymichael Patten Studio

When Chuck told me he was rewriting his book and asked if I would take a look at the foreword again, I reread the previous one, wondering if there was anything to change. I found myself re-reading his entire book, settling back into his words the way you relax into a pool of warm water: supported, free, buoyed up. At the end, I thought the same things about his work and his teaching that I had always thought, but more so.

While I was figuring how to write that down, I talked to some of his colleagues and former students, asking what of his work remained with them after they had stopped studying with him. They mentioned many things, but as with my own experience, primarily they said that what they learned had touched every part of their core beliefs about acting—had become so thoroughly absorbed that it had shaped who they were as performers. This work will stay with you forever; even better, it will keep working on your behalf as long as you do the exercises. So dive in.

I first met Chuck Jones when I was a young director coaching an actress for an audition for the Actors Studio. Chuck was her partner. Both of them were more experienced than I, so I was nervous. But I blossomed while working with Chuck. He may not have known it, but he was teaching even then, simply by the way he put his whole concentration on someone: with open attention, without judgment, listening for the essentials. Guess what? My notes to these two actors improved, because I began to pick out the essentials of what I was trying to say—because that's what Chuck was responding to.

I've seen that kind of attention when he was talking to a new student, who complained, "I've never been able to breathe right and act at the same time." Chuck zeroed in on this fellow and said, "What is breathing right? There's no special voice-class breathing or proper acting breathing. One of the ways we know what's happening with people is how they take a breath."

I could see the actor's face soften as it dawned on him that Chuck's work wasn't going to be the typical voice-class hokum. Instead, the work emphasized connecting the actor's voice to his or her emotional life. That's what we all recognize as truthfulness.

So I've sent Chuck many students over the years, saying to them, "If you think this work has nothing to do with your acting, you're wrong. Do the exercises and your acting will get better." And it does. Actors come away from his work more in touch with themselves, more relaxed, more deeply connected emotionally, more responsive to their core, acting selves.

I hope I'm communicating what a terrific teacher Chuck Jones is and what a boon his approach is to the actor. If you can't study with him directly, or if you have worked with him and need a reminder, this book is for you.

PREFACE

BY KATIE BULL

Chuck Jones invited me to share my personal vocal journey as a student and as a teacher. To be invited by one's mentor to talk about personal experience is an extraordinary honor.

I am grateful to Chuck for the work to which he introduced me over two decades ago. I was a scared, sixteen-year-old freshman when we first met—a theater arts and acting major at the State University of New York at Purchase. I had come to acting training from an experimental dance and jazz singing background, and I kept wishing there could be a more physical approach to the process of acting. The voice work with Chuck was the bridge—the "missing link"—to the visceral realm of spontaneous, unpredictable acting where connecting to a released breath equals the present moment of expression. Indeed, as I became more vocally connected, many aspects of the acting craft started to work for me. My whole body became engaged in listening, observing, experiencing the other person and responding. A whole unpremeditated, interactive world opened up; intuition, and the joy of doing plays, returned.

Two decades after learning what I call the "core" exercises, they are still the same, and anatomy still dictates the sequence. That's the beauty of this work: it is based upon the organic design of the human animal. The sequence leads you into encountering where you are vocally and emotionally trapped. That's why, when I teach, I emphasize doing the full sequence and not skipping. However, I have made adaptations and integrated elements from my knowledge of the voice through jazz singing, postmodern dance improvisation, Iyengar Yoga, Contact Improvisation, and the Laban Effort/Shape system of movement. These are all compatible ways of finding alignment for deeper breathing and impulse release. Chuck always used to say, "Make it your own."

I went on to study several other crafts of acting, always finding that an aligned, alert, energized, and breath-connected instrument was the way to remain truthful within the various craft structures presented. Whether you are an actor who initiates work on a script in a primal, intuitive way or one who chooses to analyze a script intellectually first, this work is essential. My advanced classes are now called "Vocal Integration Forums." Voice work must integrate with your particular craft of acting; if it doesn't, something is not working. You can identify the obligations to the text, you can score the script, you can scan, grasp rhetoric, emphasize operative words. But in the final moment of truth, if you are not breathing and supporting the release of a full vocal impulse, the work is not alive. It's all in your head. And it just isn't interesting.

In this revised and updated book, Chuck has chosen to include some contributions from a new generation of vocal production coaches, all of whom trained with him. This work can be taught in a myriad of styles, with numerous emphases, and for a wide range of uses. For myself, the vocal honesty, range, and power I first heard in Chuck's class over twenty years ago propelled me into a deeper dedication to the theater, and I have chosen to focus on training professional actors. If, to rephrase Shakespeare slightly, the play is the thing that catches the conscience of the king, well, that's what I want to support as a professional vocal-production coach. I want to support actors in plays that have at their essence vibrant truth, whatever the writing style, whatever the performing style. Truth is what this world needs now. Artists change lives and societies. In theater, stories wake us up to what we care about, or might not have realized we care about.

The anthropologist Margaret Mead famously said, "Never doubt that a small group of people can change the world." Theater, television, and film ensembles are the groups that can have an impact. But as a player within an ensemble, the only way to get an audience to listen is to make your voice heard. Toward that end, Chuck restores playfulness to voice work. He writes as he teaches: in a direct, unpretentious, no-nonsense manner. He offers the gift that vocal growth and change are attainable through the ownership of self-coaching skills, that they are part of reclaiming the body's wisdom. Thank you, Chuck.

You can have a potentially great acting instrument, experience deep emotions, be physically expressive, but if your voice is limited, if it is restricted by accumulated bad habits, you are incomplete as an actor. It is no coincidence that the single greatest acting influence on Stanislavisky was the opera singer Chaliapin, whose masterful acting and magnificent voice embodied for the creator of the famous System the absolute ideal of the great actor.

—David Garfield

1

WHAT TO EXPECT

I truly hope there's something in this book that helps you with your goals as an actor.

At the very least, I hope it will point you in the right direction. To me, the bottom line is to learn new things and, at the same time, make sure that this knowledge takes you where you want to be as a performer.

You really can't afford to be unintelligent about this. Stay open, but by all means look at the results. If what you are doing in actor training, including voice work, is not bringing you closer to being like the actors you admire, you need to think about your training.

What will my approach to voice training do for you? It will make you a much better actor. This, of course, will also depend on your understanding of the work and your ability to do it consistently. It will also depend on the state of your voice (and your vocal awareness) at this moment. After all, each one of you is different, and each of you has different vocal problems and strengths. People also have varying levels of ambition and discipline. So the results will be unique for each person.

But I can promise you this: If you read and understand this book and do the exercises on a regular basis, ten to fifteen minutes every day, your voice will improve a great deal. And it will be *your voice*, not an imitation of someone else's voice.

Actors who follow my advice have often told me that:

- Their voices improve in power and range;

- They have more vocal stamina;

- They are more focused in their acting;

- The honesty of their acting has grown and, in fact, their ability to act well has strengthened;

- Their auditions have gotten better results;

- Other people often respond to them in new ways. Women especially tell me they are taken more seriously. Men often tell me that people seem more receptive to them and find their manner of speaking more personal, more connected to their emotions.

This may seem too good to be true. But these are real comments from actors I have taught.

But let me *stress* that there is no magic here. The exercises are not miracles—just very effective, if done regularly. The vocal work I ask you to do follows a very natural process of development. The exercises are physiologically sound: Your voice will grow in stages, much like a seed grows when it is placed in the soil. I also use many images, so that the actor's imagination can help bring about these physiological changes. And this approach does work; I have seen it work for thirty years with thousands of actors.

My approach is based on my fifteen years of acting professionally and on personal experiences teaching privately, in studios, and in conservatory Bachelor of Fine Arts and Master of Fine Arts programs. This is not a "middle-of-the-road" approach to voice training, and there are those who will not agree with my methods. But the important thing, to me, is plainly and simply the results you achieve. No matter how terrific an approach seems to be, if it doesn't yield good and reliable results for you, it is not constructive.

Finally, my method is very much a cut-to-the-chase approach. This book contains the quickest, most efficient exercises I know. I have taken out anything that I feel is not important, of minor interest, or counterproductive to your progress.

VOICE TRAINING, NOT SPEECH TRAINING

Let me tell you a little bit more about voice work.

In many countries, voice and speech are taught together by the same teacher. In the United States, the two are often taught separately and by different specialists. Many actors are confused by the differences between voice and speech work. An actor once telephoned me and said, "My acting teacher told me to work on my voice, so I want to take your speech class." I explained to him that I teach voice, and that voice training is not the same as speech training. Often, people also confuse vocal production with singing. Of course, you have one voice, but talking and singing are quite different. (By the way, most singers who have worked with me on vocal production have told me that their singing has improved.)

Voice training primarily deals with the production of vocal tone: The range, openness, expressiveness, and flexibility of the actor's voice. Speech training concentrates primarily on articulation, dialect, and scansion. They do, of course, overlap: Both often incorporate breathing, physical relaxation, and emotional work. And both kinds of training are equally important to the actor.

But vocal exercises accomplish two distinct and vital goals for the performer: They develop the vocal instrument and they put the actor in touch with his or her emotional center. In other words, the actor learns to allow the voice to express his or her emotional life when it is appropriate or desired.

This approach to voice training is generally based on a method devised by Iris Warren, a renowned British voice teacher who passed away in 1963. I first learned her exercises from Kristin Linklater, founder of The Working Theater, which trained voice, acting, and movement teachers during the 1970s, and I am deeply grateful to Kristin for this initial training and for pointing me in the direction of teaching voice.

Over the years I have explored many other approaches to voice training—some interesting and some quite strange. However, I realized ultimately that I could use all of my experience as an actor and teacher to make this particular approach my own and, in my opinion, produce more concrete results than any other method with which I have come in contact.

CLEAR GOALS

Training your voice is like learning any new skill. You cannot study voice passionately for a certain period and then stop. Indeed, you can never learn voice training; you can only continue to practice and explore it. Voice training will become more and more interesting to you, and the major benefits will continue, only as long as you continue to practice. The key to successful vocal training is consistency.

Over the years I have learned two important facts:

- The exercises must be clear. The individual goals of each exercise must be understandable to the student;

- The exercises must produce very quick results. Progress must be experienced from the start.

Thus one of my goals as a teacher has been to develop time-efficient exercises—productive and fast-working. Over the years, in fact, I have considerably changed the exercises I use in order to make them more understandable and accessible. What is more, the voice workout presented in this book has been especially formulated, in terms of length and sequence, to support the contemporary American style of acting and actor training. I've provided the basics of voice training in a simple—although not simplistic—regimen known to produce results.

As you train your voice, I hope one of your goals will be to change lifelong physical habits of containing excessive tensions in the body. These habits usually result in vocal limitations. You, like most of us, have probably been reinforcing poor vocal habits (without knowing it) for much of your life, and it will take daily, regular work to bring about change. Still, habits can work for you as well as against you. This book is about forming new, beneficial ones.

SELF-RELIANCE

But can you learn voice training from a book? Yes! That, obviously, was part of my overall goal as an author. In New York, I have often taught professional actors the basic and second-level work in a one-year voice training program; I have distilled that basic workout for presentation in book form, and it covers all the major areas of vocal development. The twenty exercises presented in these pages can be self-taught and used by both beginners and advanced students. And this workout will change your voice.

I believe it's critical for actors to understand all the elements of their craft and be able to work on them by themselves. Sometimes, it seems to me that voice and acting teachers intentionally try to keep their work mysterious. When this happens, actors feel they must study forever with this or that particular teacher or stop doing the work altogether. The trouble is, the more mysterious voice training seems, the less able actors feel to master it. This makes it practically impossible for them to work on their own. This can also result in becoming dependent on the teacher.

When you yourself understand what you are doing and why, you can take responsibility for your work and change whatever you feel needs to be improved. Every time you take on a new role, you will feel secure enough to explore it through your voice, expand your performance, and realize the part to its fullest potential.

Voice training is about feeling confident that your vocal instrument will respond to the emotion you are trying to express and not in any way interfere with your acting process. In my teaching, I distinguish between being "in control" and being "in charge." Voice training is not about controlling the sounds you make. It is about being confidently in charge of them. If something starts to go wrong with your voice, as a professional actor you should know how to fix it. Then you are in charge. The more confident you feel, the freer both your voice and your acting will become.

Toward that end, I want each actor to understand clearly what he or she is doing and why. Again, there's no magic here—just solid results if you make an effort to grasp the purpose of each exercise and do some regular, serious, but not endless, work on yourself.

As a teacher, I've had to look very hard at the results I achieve. Often I've had to try different exercises, create new ones, and eliminate others in order to accomplish what was needed to serve the student.

As I've said, many people disagree with my approach, but it works. My students (and they are all different) have proven that to be true.

PRACTICAL, EFFICIENT EXERCISES

You can do these exercises in ten or fifteen concentrated minutes a day and you will get the results you want. Do *all* the exercises, not just the ones you like or think necessary. They all support and build on each other. I've eliminated many standard exercises, but the ones that remain are important, even if at first they don't seem to be.

Once you are comfortable with this work and have noticed some improvement, you can settle into a basic, regular routine. You will find it feels good (and you will miss the routine if you don't do it). Practicing regularly is critical for an actor, just as it is for a dancer or musician. In the beginning, as you go through your day, you will probably reinforce old habits. So to change, and integrate the new vocal habits into your life and career, you need to do a vocal workout each day.

Naturally, if you are preparing a vocally demanding role, it would be advantageous to do additional voice work; I've had much success with the idea of doing two, short (ten-minute) warm-ups a day, temporarily, while you're training for a role. But you should build up gradually. And remember, even though I say to do the workout in the right sequence, at any time you're comfortable you can throw in some additional "silent" exercises—where you make no sound.

Don't expect to keep up this intensive work forever. But as a regular routine, concentrate on keeping yourself in basic, good, vocal shape. That way you'll be in good condition for interviews and auditions.

I will say the following many times in this book, as I do when I'm teaching. It's very important to:

- Concentrate while doing the exercises. Doing them in a mechanical, off-handed, or distracted manner will accomplish little and certainly develop no awareness of how you are using your instrument;

- Understand what you are trying to accomplish with each exercise and concentrate on it.

Doing the exercises in a focused way for ten or fifteen minutes will produce more positive results than a one or two-hour, generalized, unfocused workout.

Do you believe it? Think about it. I've found it to be true: Quality in this work is much more important than quantity. And this exercise routine is one of the keys to making this work a permanent part of your life.

CHANGE AND GROWTH

In many universities where I've worked, the speech teacher often recorded the students on tape at the start of the freshman year and then again later in the spring. Although the purpose was to judge the speech, you could not help noticing changes in the voice. When the students listened to their voices at the end of the year, they were amazed at the improvements they heard.

I don't usually encourage students to listen to themselves on tape; the work is more internal than that. But listening to your voice occasionally—perhaps once or twice a year—can help if you don't get obsessed with this as a standard (don't judge yourself by your message on the answering machine; it rarely sounds much like yourself and can be quite misleading). Just read something into a tape machine as naturally as you can and listen to it later. But remember that this is a somewhat artificial situation and you're likely to be a bit self-conscious. You're not only listening to the tone of your voice but also to your rhythms and inflections—and probably not with a professional machine. Keep your sense of humor and don't get stuck on this.

Still, it's the internal experiences that are most important with this work. You will learn to do the exercises with a new awareness of yourself, and this awareness will eventually become quite developed. You will be able to sense when a part of your body is tense, when you are not breathing, and when your voice is not releasing. Essentially, you will know what's going on with your body and your voice without concentrating only on them. That's what will enable you to carry this voice work over to performance. After all, you can't make the play or film about your voice. Your subtext is not, "What's going on with my voice?" But if you are acting well, you will be in a state of "super awareness" of many things, including your voice. This heightened awareness is part of your job.

Howard Stein, one of my terrific colleagues and for many years a professor at Yale School of Drama and Columbia University, once told me a story about the great Laurette Taylor, who in 1944 originated the role of Amanda, the eccentric Southern mother in Tennessee Williams' The Glass Menagerie. During the pre-Broadway tryout in Chicago, an innocent, stage-struck student ran backstage after a performance and asked, "Miss Taylor, when you do Amanda, are you really Amanda?"

"Christ, no, dearie," Taylor quickly responded. "I'm an actress."

Like Laurette Taylor, you don't forget you are acting; you don't become lost in your role or become another person. You know where the edge of the stage is, where your mark on a film set is, and if you are using your voice correctly.

Whenever you have an opportunity to study voice with a good voice teacher, I hope you will take advantage of it. Professional actors usually know what they need to work on, and they also know whether a particular teacher or method is helping them. In the course of your career, I hope you will be confident enough to take what you need from each teacher you consult.

I feel that the exercises featured in this book are compatible with any effective voice-training class you might find in the United States or England. These exercises are also compatible with various acting approaches. As I said earlier, ever since I began teaching, I've wanted the voice work to make my students better actors. I do not want this work to interfere in any way with your genuineness as a performer. I also want the work to be practical. The exercises can be accomplished in a relatively brief period of time, and it doesn't take forever to hear and see results. I say "see," because this work will improve more than the sound and range of your voice. Your sense of yourself—and others' perceptions of you—will change for the better, onstage and off.

So I hope you will take what you can from this book. And I hope this book will open your eyes to new ways of both training the voice and becoming a more honest actor.

Having something to say and a voice to say it with—
grounded, open, human, and verbal, in life and onstage.

—David Farkas

2

THE ACTOR'S VOICE

When I was teaching at the California Institute of the Arts in the 1970s, I was surprised to find that many of my students thought they didn't need voice training because they intended to work in television and film. They assumed that voice training dealt only with stage projection. I realized then that before they could benefit from my classes, I needed to explain what voice training is all about.

Voice training isn't just about projecting the voice from the stage, although actors who work to develop their vocal instrument automatically increase their capacity to be heard. And voice training is far from the dogmatic, repetitious, irritating type of work associated with creating a "stagy" voice.

Voice training is about being *expressive*.

Actors today must be able to use their voices in a challenging variety of situations: In small theaters, huge barn-like arenas with harsh amplification, in television studios, on feature-film sound stages, and at on-location film sites. Actors may work in theaters where electronic amplification blows the voice out of human proportion, and in places where there is no sound enhancement at all. One day an actor may have to record lines in a studio, in a situation completely unrelated to the scene in which his or her image will finally appear; the next day that same actor may have to give a live interview on a television talk show.

It is impossible (even if it were desirable) to employ a different voice or vocal technique for each of these environments. But in each case the actor needs his or her voice to be fully responsive, with the appropriate quality, range, and level of loudness and emotion. Especially emotion. An actor's job is to express every kind of emotion, in virtually every kind of environment imaginable, whenever he or she chooses or is called upon to do so.

Many actors are known for having a "beautiful voice," a "stage voice," a "cute voice," a "funny voice," or a particular sound they have been taught to copy. Sally Struthers used a little squeak in the popular television series *All in the Family*. Richard Burton's voice was so "beautiful" that occasionally it got in his way, I believe.

Indeed some actors like the idea of having a voice that is attention-getting or idiosyncratic. Think of the offbeat sounds of Carol Channing and Fran Drescher. Such voices can attract a lot of notice, but their odd quality can end up being a liability, making it impossible for the actor to be cast as a normal human being. One actress who had a funny vocal twist came to me to "fix" it because she was consistently being typecast as a kook. She remembered the moment in her first performance when she got a laugh on a straight line merely because of the sound of her voice, and she had been relying on this vocal eccentricity ever since. Eventually she found her voice too limiting and wanted to be more vocally honest. We worked on developing the range and power of her voice, and she soon became comfortable using many different levels in her voice for a variety of roles.

An actor's voice, then, should never stand out as a separate part of the actor's performance. The purpose of training is to make the voice an expressive part of the actor's total instrument.

Many actors reject all voice training, as if training the voice to be more expressive were somehow "phony" or artificial. Is it artificial to diet or exercise so that your body will look better? Is it artificial to eat well to maintain good health? Good training of your voice can only make you a more accomplished actor. Some people think a voice is like height: At a certain age it becomes fixed. Well, you may not be able to grow taller after a certain age, but you can always develop your voice. In fact, the voice isn't even fully mature until after age forty, and it is capable of change throughout your life. The choice does not have to be between a phony voice or no voice at all. You can always train your voice to be more resonant, stronger, more personal, and more open.

All of this will make you a better actor. However, many actors, as well as acting teachers and directors, believe that the microphone—whether onstage or just beyond camera range—will solve all vocal problems. That is a fantasy. If a voice is problematic, a microphone will amplify the problems. In fact, the problems will be more audible and distracting. A sound system, whether excellent or poor, only amplifies the voice that is already there. Amplification cannot make a lusterless voice more expressive or a weak voice more powerful.

Several seasons ago, a long-awaited play, directed by one of America's most important stage and film directors, opened on Broadway. Three famous American film stars appeared in the leading roles, a rare event on Broadway. However, even though the show was well-miked, the voices of the stars fairly ruined their acting and almost destroyed the production. During the play's most dramatic moments, the audience could be heard clearing their throats and coughing. Why?

On a subconscious level, audiences pick up all kinds of information from the way actors use their voices. In this case, vocal and emotional power was indicated but not actually present. The actors were pushing; the audience sensed the strain, and people reacted by clearing their throats. (In the same way, if an actor is holding his or her breath onstage, audience members will hold their breath, too.)

Truthfully, when actors strain while trying to produce power, whether they are using microphones or not, they communicate weakness rather than strength. Pushing can never substitute for power. When an actor wants a character to be strong, he or she must have a strong instrument. It can't be faked.

YOUR VOCAL INSTRUMENT

The purpose of the actor's voice is to communicate. Central to conveying everything the actor is thinking and feeling, the voice should have a developed range; it should be powerful and strong when necessary, personal and intimate at other times, and able to disguise feelings as well.

What happens if you are cast in a role which demands that you grow from a flirtatious, carefree youth into a violent, imperious monarch? You can adjust your attitude and your motivation. You can change your costume and alter your makeup. But unless your vocal instrument has range and resonance and is responsive, your voice will remain the same throughout your performance. Think of the result if an actress like Melanie Griffith or Mariel Hemingway tried to play Catherine the Great. Physically, both of these women look imposing and beautiful. But their voices could belong to children. (To give due credit, Hemingway has done a good job developing the resonance and range of a voice that Woody Allen once said sounded like Minnie Mouse.)

A fully trained vocal instrument is important for reasons besides acting. Actors who develop serious vocal problems because they strain weak voices risk being replaced. It costs too much money to postpone a theatrical opening or a film shoot while an actor recovers his or her voice, or gets remedial training.

But most importantly, your performance will be more effective if you are free from vocal worries, for actors must be physically released, even in extreme physical conditions, to be emotionally revealing. The actor Jeff Daniels was once preparing a demanding one-man show based on Dalton Trumbo's novel *Johnny Got His Gun*. The character has been severely injured by a landmine; he has a head, but no body, and the play's action occurs in his mind. The production, which took place at Circle Repertory Company in New York, involved unorthodox, stylized physical staging, and throughout the play Jeff had to climb all over the stage. As dress rehearsal neared, his voice began to disappear. Now, Jeff is a disciplined actor, interested in every facet of theatrical artistry, and because of previous voice work with me, he recognized a potentially serious vocal problem in the making. He asked me to observe a rehearsal to try to identify its source.

The complicated blocking, combined with the strenuous vocal demands of the part, was creating extreme physical tension in Jeff's body, particularly around his upper back and shoulders. Also, he was not breathing fully. He and I went through the blocking step by step and concentrated on eliminating the severe tension around his neck. We also made sure that the breathing was full. That solved the problem, and his voice was fine throughout the run. It was very intelligent and professional of Jeff to take care of his voice at the first sign of trouble.

As Jeff Daniels experienced, the voice can be affected by tension arising from physical strain. Tension can also come from playing strongly emotional scenes. Intense emotion creates physical tension, which in turn causes vocal problems. The actor's goal is to relax physically without reducing emotional intensity, an aim that can be achieved with beneficial voice training.

Intense emotion can get even a well-trained voice into trouble. Chris Fields, another very talented actor whom I taught, was once rehearsing to play the lead in James Duff's *Home Front* on Broadway. Chris had one very emotional scene in the last act which required him to shout "Shut up!" twenty times rapidly, with intensity. For several weeks the director rehearsed this particular scene over and over. Not surprisingly, Chris started to lose his voice.

Like Jeff Daniels, Chris knew he was headed toward serious vocal problems, but he couldn't tell the director he didn't want to rehearse anymore. This was an emergency.

We ran the scene, and I could see that every time Chris shouted "Shut up!" his neck became rigid and he had to push his voice. The more he shouted, the greater the tension in his neck. The greater the tension, the more he pushed, and the weaker and raspier his voice became. To have adequate vocal strength and yet retain his emotional intensity, Chris needed to relax his neck. Believe it or not, there are specific voice exercises that help an actor accomplish this seemingly contradictory task, and Chris concentrated on those exercises every day for several weeks. He went on to be brilliant and very moving in the role, and he was able to sustain eight performances a week for the run of the play.

Factors such as the heightened language in classical Greek plays, Shakespeare's plays, and the comedies of Molière, can also affect an actor's voice.

Many American actors can sometimes be intimidated by this material, and that reaction can cause additional tension, restricting the voice and interfering with its expressiveness. At times, the adjustments actors make to perform heightened language can be very detrimental. Students have asked me, "How do I breathe when doing Shakespeare?" They are making an artificial adjustment.

It is true that these plays contain many complicated lines, but it is always true that you can breathe anytime the thought changes. You have to be aware of the rhythms and the poetry, but at the same time be true to your acting. You don't want to sacrifice your freedom in order to honor a phony sense of "style." Again, it all boils down to your awareness of your vocal and physical instrument.

In acting, there will always be circumstances you can't control or even expect. The question is: Do you have the awareness and skills to deal with them and give a fine performance anyway? Both the ability to recognize a problem and the skills to solve it can be developed and refined, and every actor should learn to troubleshoot his or her own vocal instrument.

Indeed, when you understand how your instrument works, you will also be able to identify problems and have a good idea of how to correct them. Above all, remember that asking for help is not a sign of weakness but an indication of strength and professionalism.

CARING FOR THE VOICE

I once acted in Michael Weller's *Moonchildren* at the Royal Court Theatre in London, where the play was called *Cancer*. One scene required that I be drenched with water from head to foot. The theater was cool backstage, and the combination of cold and dampness was congesting my sinuses. I was aware of the mechanisms involved and able to troubleshoot for myself, at least enough to take the steps of drying off completely after the nightly drenching and wearing a heavy sweater between my scenes. But the most important self-help was doing additional voice exercises to keep the sinus resonators clear.

Physical ailments can interfere with the voice. Many actors have had vocal and allergy problems from the dust and molds that accumulate backstage in older theaters. In fact, Helen Hayes retired from the theater because of her allergies, although she continued to work in film and television until her death.

I once rehearsed a Broadway play at the New Amsterdam Roof on 42nd Street, a space that had hardly been used since Florenz Ziegfeld staged his *Midnight Frolics* there in the 1920s. Although historically fascinating, the theater was a nightmare as far as dust and dirt were concerned. We coughed and sneezed our way through rehearsals.

This problem is not always easily solved. It usually requires some combination of allergy medication, the ability to do helpful vocal warm-ups, keeping a vaporizer in your dressing room, or just breathing steam deeply over the sink for a few minutes while running hot water. You usually have to find your own way, but knowledge and awareness of your voice are the keys.

Although it's not commonly recognized, voice training does more than solve vocal problems: Voice training allows actors to extend their range, develop power, and create that mysterious quality known as presence. Voice training helps put actors in touch with their deepest emotional states and allows them to connect to their roles in a profound way. And voice training helps actors develop the capacity to reveal the full range of their inner lives. This sounds like a lot, but it is indeed the truth. I know of no better way to make a person into an honest, revealing, and interesting actor than to work effectively with his or her voice.

The techniques you can use to develop your own instrument, as well as more of what voice training can do for you, will be explored in the succeeding chapters.

There came a point in my training when I felt great resistance to the work. I remember Chuck telling me, "Emily, you don't have to believe anything. Just do the exercises and your voice will change."

—Emily Caigan

3

THE DAILY VOICE
WORKOUT

The secret to developing an effective voice for acting is acquiring a *subtext* during the vocal workout. "Subtext," in this instance, has a double meaning. First, you must know the purpose of each exercise and recognize its effect on your instrument. If you do the vocal exercises mechanically, without thinking about why you are doing them, you will produce a voice disconnected from your thoughts and feelings. You are better off spending five minutes on your exercises while fully present and aware of what you're doing than you are spending five hours a day mechanically repeating the sounds Huh Huh Huh.

Second, while you carry out vocal exercises you must also be aware of your emotional life. You can't be thinking about your shopping list and do the exercises. You can't "go blank" and do the exercises. You need to be aware of what you are feeling. That doesn't mean you have to sob or laugh your way through vocal exercises. You don't need to experience a profound feeling, such as rage or joy or sadness. You can have any feeling at all, even if you can't label it.

Most of us feel several different things at once. You can train yourself to be aware of all your feelings and you can try to express them all when you are doing voice exercises. Even a simple sound like Huh can have emotional content. The emotion you are feeling may be unrecognizable to a listener. However, your emotions should be present, and you should be conscious of them.

Having a subtext is a crucial habit of mind; it is the key to developing a free, responsive, natural voice that serves your acting in every situation. It is also the "trick" that produces effective, positive change in a minimal amount of time. In each of the exercises that follow, I will show you how to use subtext.

These exercises are fairly simple to carry out, but the underpinnings of each one are very sophisticated and based on specific anatomical realities. The purpose of these exercises is to relax the vocal instrument while maintaining focus and energy, which is an ideal state in which to act a role. These exercises will teach you to recognize tension in a given portion of the vocal anatomy and train your muscles to respond to the message "Release." It's hard to believe that voice training can be so simple, but I've seen it work thousands of times.

TIME AND PLACE

Do your daily workout where and when it functions best for you. Try to choose a place where the strange and sometimes loud sounds you will be making won't inhibit you.

The advantage of doing the workout in the morning is that your voice will be warmed up for the rest of the day. However, if you prefer to do the workout at night, you are better off doing it then than not at all.

If you're in a show or auditioning often, use the workout as your warm-up. Running through the workout immediately before you audition, rehearse, or perform warms up your vocal instrument and also warms up your instincts—puts you in a good frame of mind for performance. Pre-performance voice exercises are also a good antidote to that horrible feeling of simply throwing yourself into the void. (Some actors do both a complete morning warm-up and a quick version before their show). Knowing how to make your work effective is better than praying, "May the gods be with me tonight!"

SEQUENCE OF EXERCISES FOR THE DAILY WORKOUT

The workout consists of a sequence of exercises, and it's important to perform the exercises in their proper order. The sequence provides a natural warm-up and builds to more muscular exercises, and it connects the breath to your emotion, increases vocal resonance, and finally frees the voice. The sequence is designed to give you maximum effect in a minimum amount of time.

Most actors ask me how many times to do each exercise. The ideal would be to repeat an exercise until you get the result you want. That is why you have to know what each exercise is intended to accomplish. For instance, if an exercise is designed to release neck tension, repeat it until your tension is eliminated. Sometimes you may not have enough time to get the maximum effect—this is especially true in the beginning, when you are unfamiliar with the exercises and it takes longer to complete each one successfully—but ideally, that's what you are aiming for. Remember, the effect of this work is cumulative, and just as in any physical workout, the more you practice, the more efficient you will become.

Still, depending on the amount of time you have, your motivation, and your patience, I suggest you begin with eight repetitions of each exercise and change according to your individual demands. If you are playing King Lear or Medea, for example, you might want to do more voice work than you usually do.

Below, I introduce you to each exercise. As you read the full description, "walk through" the exercise with me, right where you're sitting or standing. Some people prefer to do the warm-up partially lying on the floor. This can be useful occasionally, but not on a regular basis. You need to learn to do the exercises standing and moving. In this way you can learn to integrate the freer use of your voice while acting—which is the point.

Following this section you will find condensed versions of the same exercises, which will serve as your "coach" in the weeks that follow. Each day, you can use the capsule descriptions for your vocal workout. If you find you need more detail, come back to this chapter and reread the full description. In a few weeks, each exercise will feel familiar to you.

Finally, there is a simple list of the exercises in their proper sequence. After you are thoroughly familiar with the exercises, you can use the list as a daily reminder. Soon, the sequence will be firmly embedded in your memory, and you will be able to run through the workout without referring to the text at all.

Exercises for Body Alignment

Here is an interesting observation that might help you, from the voice teacher David Wells:

> One of the important things to practice in all these exercises is the ability to notice things about your body and voice without gripping or holding your muscles in response to that awareness: Don't let attention *breed* tension.

The exercises in the workout are designed to relax the major muscles that support the vocal instrument. Relaxing major muscles prevents straining of the smaller muscles in the throat and face.

The first two exercises will teach you to release the back of your neck—one of the major problem areas in vocal production—and the spine and belly. These are the three most important areas of the body for voice production.

1. Neck Release
Imagine that your head is held up by a string attached to the ceiling. You cut the string, and let your head fall forward. Try it now, and then bring your head back up.

- Often the best way to recognize relaxation, or release, is to compare the relaxed state to its tensed counterpart. So now imagine that you are very carefully moving your head forward. You are controlling it, letting your head go forward in a very careful movement. Feel, and think about, the difference in the quality of the two neck movements: The first time you were just letting your head drop and you did not control it. The second time, you were carefully controlling the motion of your head.

- To release the back of your neck, you want to practice the first version. Try it a few times now. Again, imagine that a string attached to the ceiling is holding up your head. Cut the string, and let your head drop forward. Feel the release in the back of your neck.

- That's the whole exercise. Try it a few times. Cut the string, hold your head up, let the head drop forward. Feel the release of the muscles.

2. Curling Over

The second exercise continues from the first.

- Drop your head forward, as above. Begin to curl over, letting your shoulders and chest roll over, letting your arms dangle in front of you. Let your knees bend, and roll down, continuing to drop your head and shoulders forward: When your hands almost reach the floor, let go. Let your hands brush the floor, and simply release all your tension and dangle. Let your head bob.

- Once you're all the way down and fully released, lift your head up. Now release it again and let your head bob.

- Now, with your neck released, start to come back up; start at the base of your spine. In a continuous rolling motion, come all the way back up, bringing your head up last. This movement can be done slowly at first, but it can be speeded up as you become better at it.

- The point of this exercise is to release the spine, abdomen, and stomach muscles, and to learn to recognize the difference between a tense neck and a released neck.

- Try it again. Drop your head forward; roll downward, rounding your spine, your knees a little bit bent. At the bottom of the bend, just let go. Now lift your head up and drop it. You should feel the release in the back of the neck.

- If you don't feel the release, lift your head up again and let it go. Do it a couple of times.

- Then start to roll back upward, letting your head come up last. Don't suck in your belly coming up. This is not an aerobics exercise. Just let your belly hang out there.

- Keep your knees bent while going down and while coming up, until you are all the way up. Finish in a fully erect posture. Your body will be completely relaxed, and your spine and neck will be in alignment.

Exercises for the Vocal Passageway

The vocal passageway comprises the throat, the back of the tongue, the soft palate (the top of the throat), the front of the tongue, the jaw, and the neck. Seven exercises concentrate on stretching the muscles in this critical voice production area. These are important exercises that directly affect the sound of your voice.

3. Tongue Releaser

When you hear people say an actor's voice is "in his throat," what they are really talking about is the tongue being tense. Emotional stress makes the tongue tense up. If you've ever lost your voice, or found your voice getting very high or otherwise changing dramatically when you're emotional, it's usually because the tongue is tensing up. This is caused by old conditioning that stems from childhood. When you were a child, you learned good manners, including speaking civilly, not screaming or screeching. Instinctively you probably found that the best way to hold back emotions was to tense the bottom of the tongue. By the time you became an adult, that tension felt completely natural. But it doesn't work for actors who have a desire at times to be vocally and emotionally open.

- You learn to release the tongue by stretching it. This requires a particular movement that must be done correctly to avoid damage to the jaw joint. Be very careful with this exercise, and follow the directions precisely.

- Relax your jaw. Take one hand and gently push your jaw down and back. It's basically a diagonal movement backward. (Do not go forward; you can take the jaw out of its hinge.) If you wish, you can hold your jaw with your hand all the time you are doing this exercise.

- Having pushed the jaw down and back, now smile with your upper lips. Lift up the muscles to create a big phony smile. Put the tip of your tongue behind the lower teeth and try to stretch the middle of the tongue out to the sides.

- With the tip of the tongue still behind the lower teeth, relax the middle of your tongue. Keep your hand on your jaw; do not let your jaw come forward.

- Another, stronger version of the same exercise is to lift your head up and look toward the ceiling. As your jaw goes back and down, push it back with your hand. Put the tip of the tongue behind the lower teeth; stretch the middle out, and let it go back.

- By stretching your tongue like this, you are actually elongating and stretching your throat.

4. Big Yawn

This is actually a stretching exercise for the soft palate, which is the top of your throat, including the little moveable part in the back of your mouth where the uvula quite visibly hangs down. The soft palate is responsible for the overtone in the upper and middle resonators, or what is called the mask area around the nose and the sinuses. Think of the overtone as like a buzzing that helps your voice to carry and sound clear. Developing the overtone is very important to every actor, particularly for clarity and carrying power.

- The soft palate has to be flexible, responsive, and able to work on its own. But it is not a part of your vocal instrument that you want to use consciously when you are speaking. If you open it up consciously you will sound unnatural—a bit like Kermit the Frog on *Sesame Street*.

- The soft palate moves up and down. To stretch it, all you have to do is yawn. (Make sure your jaw doesn't come forward.) You can yawn with your mouth open or closed. The yawn stretches the top of your throat. Actually, the stretch is a little stronger with the mouth closed, which is done as if you were trying to stifle a yawn.

- Exercise both the tongue and the soft palate on a daily basis, and then forget them and let them work on their own. Don't manipulate them when you speak. Remember the weight-lifting example: You pick up the weights and do the exercises, then put them down; you don't carry them around with you all day. It's the same with the tongue and soft palate. Exercise them and then forget about them. Let them do their jobs.

5. Whispered Keh

The purpose of this exercise is to increase the muscularity of the soft palate and back of the tongue so that they will quickly and naturally respond to your impulse to speak.

- Breathe out on a **Keh** sound. Now, put soft palate and tongue together, as you would if pronouncing the Ng sound in "Ring." Breathe in on the **Keh**.

- Alternate the two sounds—breathing out and breathing in on the **Keh**. You are using no voice here, only the soft palate and the tongue. It's out on a **Keh**, in on a **Keh**.

- This may take some experimentation. Once you feel comfortable doing it out and in, do two out, two in: Two **Kehs** out, two **Kehs** in.

- If it seems difficult to breathe in on a **Keh** sound, try this: Just breathe out on a **Keh** sound, as if you were saying the word "king."

6. Ngah Ngah Sound
This is another exercise to build flexibility into the soft palate and the back of the tongue.

- Make an **Ng** sound, as at the end of the word "ring." Then make an **ah** sound. Now combine them: **Ng-ah**.

- On the **Ng** sound, you're bringing the soft palate together with the tongue, and on the **ah** sound you are separating them. Do this two times: **Ngah Ngah**.

- Continue to repeat the two.

- You can do it on slightly different pitches. Without straining, play with different notes and different parts of your voice, but in a comfortable part of your voice. With the exercise you're waking up the muscles, getting them to respond and then to release.

- To make the exercise even more effective, relax your tongue and put it out on your lower lip. Make the sound **Ngah** twice, with your tongue staying on your lower lip. You can hold it there if you choose. This is like adding weights to the barbell, making the exercise more difficult and more effective.

Tongue Relaxer

This is a simple, very effective exercise to relax the tongue, which will add clarity to your sound. You are dealing with the whole tongue, from the very back to the very tip. A relaxed tongue will feel heavier, probably thicker, and maybe even too big for your mouth. That's only because you are used to keeping it tense.

- Put the tip of your tongue on your lower lip and think about relaxing your tongue. Without forming a word, let out a sound, like **Huh**. Let the sound come out without doing anything to your tongue. Don't let it pull back or tense up. Just let the tongue stay on your lower lip. It will feel awkward because you're not used to it.

- Let the **Huh** sound come out. It's easier if you let a little air come out before the sound starts. When you let out just a bit of air, an exaggerated aspirant, an "H" sound, comes out after it. Keep your tongue lying on the lower lip.

- Repeat the exercise using different vocal pitches. These should be easily voiced pitches, without straining. Put the tip of your tongue on your lower lip, be very conscious about relaxing it, let out a little air, and make an unformed **Huh** sound. Let the sound be whatever feels comfortable in your voice. Practice keeping the tongue really relaxed.

- As you do this exercise, you will feel your tongue becoming thicker and heavier. The sound you make during the exercise is a very weak sound, but the end result is a fuller speaking voice. But take note that the change you hear may be only subtle at first.

- The most important part of this exercise is to be conscious of what you're trying to do. You have to think about relaxing your tongue even as you do it.

8. Jaw I (Relaxation)

You see actors in film close-ups with jaw tension all the time: It's the teeth-clenching, jaw-flexing, Clint Eastwood–school of acting. Unfortunately, when tension is held in the jaw, the voice is constricted, and so is expression.

- The secret of keeping the jaw relaxed while speaking is to relax the back of the neck. The back of the neck is a very defended area of the body. It is often tense, and tension shortens the neck muscles. If you can relax your neck, your jaw will automatically be relaxed.

- Take one hand and gently move your jaw back and forth diagonally, a down-and-back movement—not strictly up and down. You're basically testing to see if the jaw muscles are released and encouraging them to release further. Continue to move your jaw back and forth very easily, and think about releasing the back of your neck.

- When your jaw and neck begin to feel loose, try making a simple **Huh** sound while you're doing it.

- Try using different pitches for this sound as you continue to move your jaw, keeping the back of your neck relaxed.

- This can be a frustrating exercise for people with extremely tight jaws. Some people find that when they try to move the jaw it clenches even further. Stay with it and gently persevere. It takes time, but at some point you will be able to move your jaw fluidly back and forth.

- Some people find it easier to do this exercise while lying down. You might try that and see if it helps you. (If you are lying down, the muscles in back of the neck should feel very released, because no muscles are being used to hold the head up.) With your knees up and your feet flat on the floor, lie in a comfortable position. Gently move the jaw back and forth.

- Remember, you can never force a release. All you can do is coax yourself and send a message by thinking: "Relax the jaw, relax the back of the neck." It may take several weeks before you actually notice a result and hear a more open quality in your voice.

- Some people clench their jaws while they sleep, which means the jaw is going to be tense when they wake up. If this sounds like you, do this jaw exercise when you get up in the morning. Very occasionally, people also have problems with poor jaw alignment, which requires help from a dentist.

- Continue practicing this exercise and you will be able to effect a change.

9. Jaw II (Isometric)

This is an isometric exercise that can help relax a very tight jaw. In isometrics, two parts of the body push against each other with equal force, so that neither one moves.

It's *very* important to do this exercise correctly or you can damage the jaw joint. The exercise is in five steps:

- Put your left fist against your left cheek, right next to your mouth. Push your fist toward your cheek into the jawbone and push your cheek toward your fist. Neither one should move. Hold it for about seven seconds—and release.

- Repeat the exercise on the other side—the right fist against your right cheek. Push toward your jawbone, with no movement. Hold it for seven seconds—and release.

- Grasp your chin with your hand and push down; push up with your chin at the same time. Hold it for seven seconds—and release.

- Put your fist underneath your jaw, at the chin. Push up with your fist; and push down with your jaw. Hold it for seven seconds—and release.

- End the sequence by moving your jaw back and forth.

Exercises to Connect Voice to Breath

There are only two ways that human beings can produce sound: You can produce your voice with muscular tension, or you can connect your voice to your breathing and let your breath produce the sound. We have discussed why sound carried on the breath is by far the most useful for an actor's voice. These are the exercises that help you feel the connection between your breath and your voice.

10. Centering

Lie on the floor on your back, keeping your knees bent. Place one hand on your lower abdomen, or belly. Try to release those muscles; let go of any tension in them. Your breath will seem to drop down into your abdomen. In reality, the diaphragm is being freed because you're not holding in your belly. (The breath, of course, does not really enter your abdomen.)

- Now employ an image: Think of your breath going into your lower belly—you're just letting it go in there. While you're lying on the floor, you're not making any intense physical exertion, so you need very little breath. You want the breath to go down into the belly. Then just let it come out, just as you do when you're sleeping. Don't control it or sustain it. You want to let go. You are relaxing the muscles, allowing the breath to go into your belly and letting it leave without controlling it.

- One of the usual mistakes an actor makes when doing any exercise is to push the breath out. You don't need to do that. Another common mistake is holding your breath, so that you do a kind of slow, controlled breathing, perhaps counting while you breathe in and out. That's not what you are aiming for here. You just want to let it flow in—and then let it leave without any control.

- Next, sit up on the floor and cross your legs in whatever sitting position feels comfortable. Place one hand on your lower belly and see if you can let the breath drop into the belly and then escape. Work with it until you feel some progress. It may take five minutes or more before you can actually release those muscles.

- After you've completed the exercise in a sitting position, try doing it standing up. Keeping your knees relaxed, put a hand on your lower belly, and see if you can release the muscles and let the breath in easily.

- Many people, especially women, feel that when they release their abdominal muscles their belly becomes much larger, almost as if they were pregnant. You should know that although the belly feels enormous, in reality the visible change is minimal. It feels big, but it does not look like you are slouching or suddenly developing a pot belly.

- While you're doing the breathing exercise, let yourself tune into whatever you're feeling. It doesn't have to be anything profound. Just acknowledge the feeling, even if you can't label it, and let the breath go in and easily come out. There's a point to this: To train the voice to be connected to your emotional life. The key to having your voice be emotionally revealing is breathing freely while you are in touch with your emotional life. Without awareness of your emotional state, your voice will be disconnected, placed artificially, and manipulated. It's simple once you get the hang of it.

11. Sound Vibration

Now think of this image: Your sound actually comes from deep down inside your belly (we know this isn't true, of course; sound comes from your vocal cords). Employ the image that the sound is coming from deep down in your body. You can picture it, and it will be an effective way to get the voice connected and supported by the breath. Basically, you are working with two images: First, of the breath going down into your belly, and secondly, that the sound is also coming from down there. As you work with those images, you will make a connection between your voice and your breath.

- Pretending for the moment that your voice is coming from your belly—that it's deep down inside—let out a little unformed sound, something like **Huh**. Just imagine that tiny **Huh** sound coming from your belly. Also produce that sound using a couple of other vocal pitches, without straining. You can place your hand on your belly, if you like.

- You are putting things together at this point: Breathing without manipulating the breath, without any pushing or any controlling; imagining that the sound of your voice is coming from deep inside your belly; working with an image, even if part of your brain is saying "This isn't right." Play around with easy pitches on the **Huh** sound, and see if you can feel the connection between your breath and your voice.

- After you have gained some practice, combine this exercise with Exercise 2, Curling Over: While playing with the sound **Huh** on different easy pitches, drop your head forward and, with a rolling motion along your spine, bend all the way over. Let go when you bottom out, exaggerating the release of tension; then pick your head up and release it again. With your head bobbing, feel the release in the back of your neck. Then, with your neck and belly muscles released, "roll" back up, all the time continuing to produce the **Huh** sound employing different pitches.

- In your daily workout, do this exercise in all three positions—first lying down, then sitting up, and finally standing up. Doing the combinations introduces you to the feeling of producing sound from a relaxed instrument. This is a natural process that you want to carry over into your everyday life. It will take some time and some practice, but you will be able to apply it to your work.

- With these exercises you're training your body not to interfere with the natural process of producing sound on the breath. Eventually, the body will recognize that this is a more efficient way of expressing sound and will welcome the change.

Exercises for the Resonating Chambers

Your whole body is a resonator. The vocal cords are like the strings of a violin, and your body is like the violin's hollow wooden case. Violin strings and vocal cords make only a very tiny sound by themselves. The sound is increased as it resonates through the body. The whole body actually vibrates. If you are aware of it, you can sometimes feel sound vibrating all the way down to the tips of your toes. We have seen how certain key areas, called resonating chambers, are known to increase sound: The chest, for example, has its most dramatic effect on the lower parts of your vocal range; the hard palate and the sinus area affect the middle range and enable your voice to carry; and the top of your skull, the highest resonator, helps you produce the highest part of your range.

- Together, these major resonators contribute to the full range of your voice. If you use only some and not others, your range will be limited. If you use all, but they are weakly developed, your range will be weak.

- But if you practice sending sound to the resonating chambers, starting with your chest and going all the way up to your skull, your range will be fluid and connected. In this way you're covering all the areas of your voice and, with time, each will become fully developed.

- In the next group of exercises, we're going to practice producing sound from these resonators. The amount of vibration you will get in various resonators depends on how relaxed the body is, how toned the muscles are, and whether you are comfortable sending sound to that particular area.

- For example, women often avoid producing sound through the chest resonator in an effort to sound more feminine or more socially acceptable. Men tend to avoid using the upper resonators because they fear showing vulnerability; they try to hold their voices down in the chest area where it feels stronger. Actors, men and women, need to become comfortable sending sound through the body's major resonators, so that they have a complete instrument with which to communicate.

12. The Chest

The chest is the power source of your voice, supplying the entire bottom half of your range. This is a very large resonator, and you can often get much more from it than you're accustomed to using.

- Lift your head up just a little bit, a couple of inches. Let your mouth drop open, as if you'd gone to sleep. Just let it fall open. Make an **Aahhh** sound—a sigh, with a downward inflection, going through the chest area. Let a little bit of air come out first, before you produce the sound; this will help keep your tongue relaxed. A little bit of air, then a sigh—and make it a very long sigh: **Aaaaahhhhhhhh.**

- Place your hand on your chest and feel the vibrations. This is the lower part of your voice. The lower the resonator is, the lower your pitch. The low sound you are working with right now is going down into your chest. So make a downward inflection on the **Aahhh** and let the sound go into your chest.

- Now lift your arms above your head and let them drop—just let them go. Try to let your voice drop just as you did with your arms. Just let it go, dropping that sound out of your throat and down into your chest.

13. The Hard Palate

The hard palate, the roof of your mouth, is a round, hard surface in front of the soft palate. The soft palate moves, but the hard palate does not. The hard palate is an important resonator for your voice, but how can you exercise it?

- Put your finger in your mouth, but without touching anything, and blow air on your finger. Feel the breath touch your finger. Now, send a **Huh** sound onto your finger. Do you feel a vibration?

- The hard palate is a very small resonator compared to the chest, so it may take a couple of weeks of repeating this exercise before you become sensitive to the vibration. But the sound is vibrating even if you can't actually feel it yet.

- Continue to do the exercise, sending a **Huh** sound onto your finger. Eventually, you will be able to feel the sound on your finger. Now continue the exercise without putting your finger in your mouth; just send the **Huh** to the front of the roof of your mouth, and let it come out. Basically, you're placing the sound in this tiny littlie area of your voice. When I do this exercise I feel the effect more in the front half of my mouth, rather than in the back.

- Because the hard palate is a higher resonating area, your pitch is also higher. Play around with the two different sounds you produced in the hard palate resonator and in the chest resonator (Exercise 12, above). Go from one to the other, and feel the difference in pitch and in where the sound is vibrating in your body.

14. The Sinuses

The sinus resonators are on either side of your nose. If you put two fingers right next to your nostrils, you will feel that the flesh there is soft. That's the resonating area we are talking about. This exercise will increase the blood circulation to the tissue in that area, which in turn will drain the sinuses. When the sinus cavities are well drained, vibration will increase, and your voice will carry better.

- You can use various sounds for this exercise, but let's stick with the simple, unformed **Huh** sound. You're going to do this on different pitches. Again, because the sinus resonators are even higher in your body, the pitches will be higher than in the previous exercises.

- On different pitches, send the sound **Huh** out of your mouth (not through your nose). Put two fingers alongside each of your nostrils and massage the sinuses as you do different pitches. Just gently move your fingers up and down.

- Go up a scale with easy notes. Go higher than the pitch you used when vibrating the roof of your mouth. All the while, massage the area on either side of your nostrils. You won't feel a lot of vibration while you do this; you will mainly feel the pressure of your fingers. But after you finish you may hear more resonance coming from that area when you speak.

- This is tricky. You only consciously use the sinus resonator while doing the exercise. When you are actually speaking, you do not ever want to isolate sound in this area. The purpose of the exercise is to help the sinuses drain, which helps keep the sinus cavities hollow, which in turn gives your speaking voice more resonance and clarity.

15. The Nose

The nasal resonator, together with the sinus resonator (which you worked on in the previous exercise) is called the vocal mask. These two resonators are responsible for a vocal overtone throughout your entire range that gives the voice clarity, brilliance, and carrying power. It's a kind of buzzing in your voice.

- Wrinkle up your nose and send a **Ne-Ne-Ne** sound right into the nose: **Ne-Ne-Ne**. I know, it's a very strange sound, an aggressive, strident one. Do it anyway: **Ne-Ne-Ne**, right through the nose. You can do it on various pitches.

- You will probably feel some tightening in your throat, so be careful not to overdo the exercise. Your goal is to produce the high-pitched **Ne-Ne-Ne** sound while your neck and tongue are completely relaxed. Slowly moving your head from side to side as you do the exercise will help coax the back of the neck to relax.

- You can also do the exercise with your tongue out on your lower lip in a relaxed, loose, soft manner.

- You want the **Ne-Ne-Ne** sound to be in your nose, not in your throat. You will probably go through a phase where the sound is half in your nose and half in your throat. If you continue to do the exercise while consciously relaxing your neck and tongue, eventually you will be able to do it through your nose. Practice this exercise only a few minutes at a time.

16. The Skull

The last major resonating chamber is the skull, which you can think of as the very top of your voice. Voice work in this area will strengthen the entire voice and extend your upper range. For men, using this upper resonator produces a very distinct sound, the *falsetto*. Female singers call this their "head voice," but I discourage you from thinking of the voice in this way. I find that singing terms such as "head voice" and "chest voice" are limiting for actors. I would prefer that you think of different resonating chambers, all connected.

- In this exercise, you want to send a high, long **EEEE** sound, on different pitches, up into your highest resonator. Bear in mind that the higher the pitch, often the greater the tension in your body. One excellent way to prevent your body from tensing up during the exercise is to curl over (as in Exercise 2), rolling down the spine, while you're doing it. So drop your head forward, roll down your spine, curl all the way over and let go at the bottom of the curl. Allow your head to bob and your neck to be absolutely free.

- Now, create the **EEEE** sound while you are dangling in that position. If you do the **EEEE** exercise from this fully relaxed position, you will not have to reach physically for the notes. Stay down for a minute or two; then, curl back up along the spine.

Exercises to Liberate Your Voice

In the previous group of exercises, you practiced sending sound to specific resonators of your body. In this final group you will let the sound go wherever it wants to go. You are going to practice using your body in a way that completely opens up the voice.

17. Knees Only
Try this: Begin by standing relaxed. Bend your knees a bit, and then straighten them again. As you bounce a little this way, going gently up and down, let out a very easy **Hah** sound as you bounce. If your body is very relaxed, your voice will also bounce up and down. In other words, your voice will be affected by the movement of your body. Your voice will shake. This is the kind of connection you want to make when you liberate your voice.

18. Larger Movement I
Very easily, move your knees up and down, bending your legs a little bit and then straightening them. Or jump up and down very gently. Say this line: "My name is (*your name*)."

- Let your voice respond to the physical movement. Let it shake and let it stand still.

- Now try it again, but this time while you gently bounce up and down, do whatever you can to prevent your voice from shaking. That is exactly what you want not to happen, but it will be useful to feel it done "wrong."

- Tighten your neck or tighten your belly. Sometimes you can stop your voice from shaking if you speak very quickly or use your voice very lightly. Stopping your voice from shaking while you are moving requires some kind of tension and holding, and any method you use will disengage your voice from your body.

- Again, this is the opposite of what you want to happen, and you will feel the difference. Your goal is to liberate your voice, so that it does shake when you are moving. That is when you will get the most released voice possible. When you bounce up and down, your voice should shake. That is the correct way to do the exercise.

19. Larger Movement II

While you are gently jumping up and down, letting your voice shake, very easily make a **Hah** sound with a downward inflection, and let the sigh run from the very top of your range all the way down through the bottom. Your goal is to let your voice respond freely to the physical movement of your body. Make the **Hah** sound accompanied by the physical movement. This is how you learn to produce sound in a liberated way.

- Next, repeat the same downward sigh, from the top of your range to the bottom, but do this while standing still. This should give you a sense of how it feels to use your real voice—the free voice that would shake if you were jumping. And this is the effect you want.

- Finally, do it while jumping again, and allow the voice to shake through all the resonators.

- The way to discover your real voice is to practice making any sound while jumping and letting your voice shake. If you practice using a sentence, you will have to slow it down a little bit. (You cannot do this exercise fast.)

- Once again, stand still, and repeat **Hah Hah Hah**. Your voice doesn't shake, but you stay connected.

20. Finale

The final exercise in the sequence lets you end the session performance-ready. You are going to take any piece of material—a speech, a sentence, a poem, whatever you wish—and free it up while you are doing a loose physical movement, which means that your voice will shake. You can bounce up and down, fling yourself around in a swirl, or roll around on the floor. Do any physical movement that feels loose.

- Try to act the speech *while* you liberate your body. You will probably feel very silly, but this exercise is the critical step for you to feel your voice coming out while it is fully connected to your body.

- Try alternating between physically freeing your body while saying a line of dialogue, and then standing still while saying the same line, using your voice in the same way.

- If you have trouble making the connection while you are standing still, try this: Move on the first couple of words, then stop moving and let the voice continue to come out. That way you can train yourself to use the same connected, free vocal production when you are still.

Summing up the Workout

The sequence of the vocal workout takes you from relaxing the muscles of your body, to connecting your voice to the breath and toning the vocal resonating chambers. It ends by liberating your voice. By the time you have finished the sequence, you are in full acting mode and are ready to begin. This is the workout I want you to do every day.

The secret is this: If you do the workout routinely every day you will develop a very fine vocal quality. Good vocal quality is a small goal for an actor. You want much more than that.

You want your voice to be open and honest and to serve your acting.

Never do your voice workout by "spacing out" mentally and simply repeating the exercises by rote. You have to know what you're doing and why. You have to be in touch with yourself.

If you work out with purpose and intent you will get maximum results in minimum time. Your sound will become more developed, your range extended, and your voice more open, more expressive, and more revealing.

A CAPSULE VERSION OF THE DAILY WORKOUT

Once you have accustomed yourself to the daily workout, this concisely worded version will come in handy as a guide. An even briefer version—really just a reminder list—follows this version for quick reference.

Exercises for Body Alignment

1. Neck Release

- Drop your head forward.

- Do not control the movement. Just let it go.

- Repeat until you feel relaxed.

2. Curling Over

- Let your head drop forward. Allow your torso to roll down toward your feet, letting go at the bottom. Dangle.

- Roll back up to a relaxed standing position. Do not hold the belly in.

- Allow the knees to release; bend a little bit.

- Make sure there are two releases—the head at the start, the neck when you reach the bottom. The head should bob.

- Repeat three or four times.

Exercises for the Vocal Passageway

3. Tongue Releaser

- Place the tip of your tongue behind your lower teeth.

- Release your jaw backward (not forward).

- Roll the middle of the tongue forward, keeping the tip behind the lower teeth.

- Do not allow the jaw to go forward. Hold it with your hand. Try turning your face up, toward the ceiling.

- Repeat several times.

4. Big Yawn (Soft Palate)

- Let your jaw go back toward the back of your neck.

- Yawn or stifle a yawn, letting the soft palate rise. Do not allow the jaw to go forward, but only backward toward the back of your neck.

- Repeat several times.

5. Whispered Keh

- Breathe in and out on a whispered **Keh** sound.

- Make sure that the soft palate and back of the tongue come together on the outgoing and incoming breath. Make sure the jaw is not moving. Put one finger on the jaw to hold it still.

- Use only the soft palate and the back of the tongue to produce the **Keh** sound.

- Repeat about twenty times.

6. Ngah Ngah Sound

- The soft palate and the back of the tongue come together, as you make an **Ng** sound, followed by an **ah** sound: **Ngah**.

- The jaw should not move. Put a finger on the jaw to hold it still. Only move the soft palate and the back of the tongue.

- Repeat about twenty times.

7. Tongue Relaxer

- Put your tongue out on your lower lip. Keep the tongue relaxed, and produce a **Huh** sound.

- Let a little air come first, before the sound.

- Repeat about twenty times, on different pitches.

8. Jaw I (Relaxation)

- Very easily, move the lower jaw back and forth toward the back of your neck.

- Make sure your neck is relaxed. If your neck is relaxed, it will help the jaw relax.

- Repeat about twenty times.

9. Jaw II (Isometric)

- Hold your fist against your jaw in four positions: On the right and the left sides, then pushing down and pushing up.

- Do not allow your jaw to move. Keep it aligned.

Exercises to Connect Voice to Breath

10. Centering

- Lie on the floor on your back. Relax your abdominal muscles and let the breath go down into your belly—as low as possible.

- Let it come out again. Do not manipulate your muscles.

- Continue to allow your breath to go in and out of your abdomen, as if you were sleeping.

- Do the breathing exercise also while sitting up; then do it standing.

- Remain in each position until you feel comfortable.

11. Sound Vibration

- Pretend that the sound comes from the abdomen. Allow a **Huh** sound to come out from your belly.

- You are not using articulators. Imagine that the sound is just a very plain, unformed sound coming from your belly.

- Using different pitches, repeat about twenty times.

Exercises for the Resonating Chambers

12. The Chest

- Use an **Ah** sound. Allow the **Aahhh** to sigh in your chest.

- Lift your head slightly. Your throat is relaxed. The back of your tongue is relaxed. Your neck is relaxed.

- Repeat about ten times.

13. Hard Palate

- Open your mouth. Send **Huh** into the roof of your mouth. The pitch should be higher than a chest resonator. Put your finger in your open mouth and send a breath on to it. Then send a sound on to your finger.

- Repeat about ten times.

14. The Sinuses

- Put two fingers on either side of your nostrils and massage that area. Simultaneously, let out the same **Huh** sound as before.

- Go up and down a scale, as you continue to massage the area. Let the sound come out of your mouth.

- Keep your tongue, jaw, and neck as relaxed as possible.

- Repeat on eight to ten different notes.

15. The Nose

- Send a **Ne-Ne-Ne-Ne** sound right into the nose. The sound should come out of your nose, not your mouth.

- Let the sound spread across your face.

- Lift your cheeks up. Keep the back of your neck relaxed.

- Repeat about six times.

16. The Skull

- This is the very top of your voice. Use an **EEEE** sound and send it to the very top of your range. Try to keep your jaw released. (You can move your jaw back and forth as you send the sound).

- Keep your neck released.

- Repeat eight to ten times.

Exercises to Liberate Your Voice

17. Knees Only

- With your feet on the floor, knees bent, bounce gently up and down, saying **Hah Hah Hah**.

- Let your voice shake.

- Continue bouncing until you feel open.

18. Larger Movement I

- Bounce up and down gently, saying your name.

- Let your voice shake.

- Continue bouncing, and try to stop your voice from shaking. The goal is to recognize tension.

- Begin again, letting your voice shake.

19. Larger Movement II

- Jump up and down gently, saying **Hah Hah Hah**.

- Go through the entire range of your voice, from your lowest notes to your top note, continuing to jump on **Hah Hah Hah**.

- Let your voice shake.

- Stand still and go through the entire range again, saying **Hah Hah Hah**. Keep your neck and jaw relaxed as you go up into your high range.

- Your voice doesn't shake, but stays connected. Let the voice crack. It doesn't matter. Just keep the body released.

- Repeat a few times.

20. Finale

- Bounce up and down, fling yourself around in a swirl, or roll around on the floor. Do any physical movement that feels free and loose.

- At the same time, act a speech. Your voice will shake mightily.

- Alternate acting while moving and acting while standing still. See if you maintain the emotional connection.

A BRIEF REMINDER

I feel it's very important to learn the exercises so that they become an integral part of you and you don't have to read them each time you do them. When doing your workout, you must put your attention on yourself and not on the printed page.

Another reason to know these exercises by heart is that you never know when you might want to do them. For example, before an audition you might do a thorough workout at home; but if you have time, you might also want to do a quick one later at the audition. When you regularly do a solid workout, you can accomplish a great deal with a very short one, because your body is already conditioned and will respond quickly. If you want results, put some effort into making this daily workout your own. Then, once you are totally familiar with it, all you will need is the following brief reminder to do the correct sequence.

Exercises for Body Alignment

1. Neck Release: Drop your head.

2. Curling Over: Roll all the way down your spine and curl back up.

Exercises for the Vocal Passageway

3. Tongue Exercise: Stretch.

4. Big Yawn (Soft Palate).

5. Whispered **Keh** (Soft Palate and Tongue).

6. **Ngah Ngah** (Soft Palate and Tongue).

7. Tongue Relaxer: Tongue on Lower Lip.

8. Jaw I, Relaxation: Gently move your jaws.

9. Jaw II, Isometric: Push your fist against your jaws in four positions.

Exercises to Connect Voice to Breath

10. Centering: Feel your breath in your abdomen.

11. Sound Vibration: Connect an unformed sound to your breath.

Exercises for the Resonating Chambers

12. Chest.

13. Hard Palate.

14. The Sinuses.

15. The Nose.

16. The Skull.

Exercises to Liberate Your Voice

17. Knees Only: Bounce gently with knees only.

18. Larger Movement I.

19. Larger Movement II.

20. Finale: The Big Roll-Around.

When I auditioned for the State University of New York at Purchase, I had just finished four years of competing in Dramatic Interpretation in high school. (Which means that I took ten minutes of a play and performed all the characters. Yes: in ninth grade I actually played Blanche, Stella, Mitch, and Stanley from Tennessee Williams' A Streetcar Named Desire.) Not only had I developed bad vocal habits, I had honed them to a science. My voice was tense, controlled, nasal, and manipulated. At the audition, after my monologue, I remember all eyes in the room turned from me to Chuck. He got up and put his hand on my stomach and asked me to let the breath drop in. Huhummmah. I looked around the room. Everyone looked at Chuck. This was going to be a vocal Mt. Everest.

The voice training with Chuck was really the element that freed my acting. For the first four months, every time my breath dropped into my stomach, I cried. There had been so many years of vocally controlling my emotions, that when those muscles finally let go, there was a river. I worried for a time that I would never be able to breathe without sobbing. But gradually that freedom expressed itself in more nuanced and subtle ways. During student review at the end of the year, Chuck received a standing ovation for the mountain he'd scaled with me.

Now, many years later, I wouldn't step onstage without doing his warm-up. It's the most crucial step toward getting me centered, focused, and free.
"STEL-LAHHHHH!"

—Deborah Laufer

4

DEEPER INTO
THE WORKOUT

In an effort to relax, actors sometimes start to slouch and collapse physically. If you don't want to act in this position, you need to address your physical alignment while you're doing the exercises. This means that you have to be aware of how you are standing or moving as you are doing the exercises. What we are trying to do is to replace old habits with new, more effective ones. You also need to pay attention to your habits in your daily life. Francine Zerfas, one of the teachers I have trained, and one who has a strong movement and dance background, has written a segment for my book specifically concerning physical alignment.

Many times I have worked with women who are in various stages of pregnancy. I've always been very concerned that this work be safe for both the student and her baby, and naturally a student should consult her physician about the exercises in advance. But several of the teachers I've trained have had children, and this chapter also includes some very useful comments from both Francine Zerfas and Katie Bull concerning this issue.

ALIGNMENT By Francine Zerfas

At some time in your life, you probably heard someone say, "Stand up straight." Most likely, the reason behind this request was to encourage you to be and look more alert, respectable, and present. In this voice work, "standing up straight," or aligning yourself as it is also called, is very important. Beginning the warm-up from a well-aligned body allows the breath to flow more easily along the spine and the entire body.

What does it mean to be well-aligned and how do you achieve that?

One of the very first things you are asked to do in the warm-up is to come into aligned and active stance. In other words:

- To stand with your head centered and floating lightly on top of your spine;

- To have your shoulders squared and centered over your hips; that is, shoulders not hunched forward or pulled back;

- To have your hips over your knees;

- To have your knees centered over your feet;

- To have both feet planted gently but firmly on the floor.

You may notice that this creates a stronger presence. You are now physically more focused, open, and available to your breath and its impulses.

When trying to achieve easy and upright alignment, you will immediately begin to learn about your body. You will learn where its strengths and weaknesses are, where tensions exist, and even more importantly, your habit of breathing. Breathing is something you have done since birth; it is something your body does involuntarily. As a result, you tend not to pay much attention to *how* you breathe, because you *are* breathing. It is not that you are breathing incorrectly, but that, for reasons that aren't always apparent, you may have developed physical habits which make it difficult to breathe and speak with ease. And this can interfere with your acting.

Exercise I

When I introduce the notion of a well-aligned body to my students, I often do an exercise Chuck introduced to me when I was a student. It's called "What's wrong with this picture?"

1. Place yourself in what I describe above as a well-aligned body. Gently tuck your pelvis forward. Ask yourself: What does it feel like? What happens to your breath when your body is in this position? Is it easier or harder to breathe or take a full breath? Do you feel any residual tension as a result of the pelvis being forward? If so, try to name each tense spot. Try speaking your name and address in this position. Then ask yourself: Do either of these positions seem familiar or comfortable?

Tucking the pelvis forward usually results in the upper body collapsing, thus causing the abdominals, diaphragm, and rib muscles to shorten and tighten. In this position, it becomes very difficult to get a breath that will support what you say.

2. Now, sway your back and push your buttocks up. Ask yourself these same questions: How does it feel? What happens to the breath? Where do I feel tension? Name the tense places. Try speaking in that position. And again, are this alignment and breathing habitual?

Swaying the back causes tense and disengaged abdominals. This position forces the breath to be taken up higher in the chest, and as a result, the throat tightens.

3. The last stage of the exercise involves making the appropriate adjustments to create a well-aligned and centered body. In the pelvic tuck, the groin and lower abdominals need to relax so the pelvis can experience its natural length. In the sway back, the upper buttocks need to relax and lengthen down in order to find that centered pelvis. When this happens, the entire torso, from the base of the spine to the very top of the cervical vertebrae, will respond by lengthening. (Remind yourself to breathe, or the muscles will not be pliable.) Then ask yourself to observe any tension and notice what your breathing is like.

Heightened Observations for any Time of the Day

I often instruct my students to do what I call heightened observations of themselves, so that they can learn about their breathing and other physical habits—both those that are helpful and those that are limiting. It is useful to *observe* habits in action in order to *understand* them before making changes. Heightened observations are about you observing yourself in any context, at any time during the day, and as often as you desire.

Consider these heightened observations of your body:

1. How do you tend to *sit* during the course of the day? Do you sit with your legs crossed, for example? Do you sit with your upper body hunched over? At that moment of observation, what is your breath like in that position? What happens if you change the way you are sitting and, with ease, allow your spine to straighten by placing you shoulders over your hips

and, still sitting, plant your feet firmly on the floor? What's your breath like then?

2. How do you tend to *stand* during the course of the day? At that moment of observation, what is your breath like in that position? How does the position make you feel? Do you feel lazy, lethargic, energized, tense, or calm? Does the position affect the way you speak? Do you think it encourages you to speak quickly, without taking sufficient breath, as if you were nervous? Or does it encourage you to speak slowly, as if you weren't really interested in communicating or perhaps were too tired to do so? What happens if you change the way in which you are standing, so that you have a more centered and supported, aligned body?

Please understand that, by suggesting these observations, I am not proposing that you must adopt your daily sitting or standing to a more aligned body. You may choose to do so if you find it beneficial. As an actor, you do not want to limit the characters you play to one body posture. What is useful here is to learn about physical habits that may be limiting your breathing and its impulses, and how in various postures, you may be holding unnecessary tension that is limiting your vocal and acting work. If you adopt a hunching posture, for instance, when playing a certain character, you will need to learn how to access and support your voice while existing in that character's body.

Exercise 2

Alignment begins from the feet up. This stance is not a passive or static one, but rather as fluid as breathing, for even when we are standing still our bodies are in motion. This can be observed simply by observing your breath in the following exercise.

Begin this exercise in a well-aligned, standing position.

1. Notice where the weight of your body is.

Is the weight back on your heels or forward on your toes? Ideally, it should be in the center of your feet, easily available to shifting back or forth when you next take a step. Does shifting that balance affect your breath?

2. Notice tension that may exist in your body as you come into this stance.

Are you holding any tension in the neck? Are the ribs held tightly? Can you notice any movement of the ribs? Is that movement vertical (straight up and down), or does it fan out like a bellows? Do you automatically hold your abdomen in? If so, are you doing that continually? What about your pelvis? Your buttocks? Are they tensed? Continue observing the tension in your body all the way down to your feet.

3. Now, after all these observations, which take only seconds to complete, how are you breathing?

Where do you feel movement in your body? Are you breathing in your chest, or do you feel the breath a little lower in the body? Do you feel any movement in your belly and ribs?

For many of us, being aligned is often not our natural state. I often hear, "But it's not natural to me." This may indeed be true; reconditioning the body's responses takes time and practice. If you've ever taken a dance or yoga class or done any physical training—even playing the piano—the skills necessary for that discipline are often not your first physical instinct. We all have to train and practice, to teach our muscles to behave differently. Body alignment will make it easier for you to access your breath, build support, and develop greater tone overall in your voice.

PREGNANCY AND THE VOCAL WORKOUT
By Francine Zerfas

It is not unusual these days for women to continue acting when they are pregnant. If you are pregnant and wondering if Chuck's warm-up is something you should learn or continue to do, I suggest that first you seek your doctor's advice about what kind of physical exercise is advisable for you. Only then should you learn, or continue, the warm-up.

I taught Chuck's work throughout my entire pregnancy, because nothing with my pregnancy deterred me from physical exercise. I once worked with a student until her seventh month, although, as time progressed, modifications to various exercises were necessary; as she neared the end of her second trimester and began her third, certain movements were eliminated altogether. Below are some suggestions for modifications to the warm-up during pregnancy.

1. Rolling down and up the spine

Rolling through all twenty-four vertebrae in the spine is done to release tension in the neck and the back muscles—tension that tends to tighten the breath.

But as early as your first trimester, rolling down and up the spine will require adjustments. As your belly begins to grow, it will become increasingly difficult for you to roll through each articulated vertebra. So you should only roll down as far as that new belly will allow. Just rolling down gently as far as the first five neck vertebrae, or even a little further if you can manage it, will help release tension and invite more air into the body.

2. Shaking the body, bouncing, or gentle jumps up and down

As your pregnancy progresses, bouncing, jumping even slightly, or even shaking your body from side to side can be uncomfortable. Over time, it is also common that your breasts will become too sensitive to allow such movement. In addition, you may find that, when you jump, the weight of your belly will create some discomfort in your back or your knees. This was not true for me until quite late in my pregnancy, but each woman's situation is different. You may want, first, to see if decreasing the movement decreases the discomfort. If it doesn't, then eliminate the bouncing altogether. Movement does help to free the breath in the body, which is why we rely so much on these movements during the warm-up. But, if necessary, you can warm up with considerably less movement.

3. Chair Modification

When my pregnancy progressed to its last trimester, I began to do the warm-up while sitting in a chair. I sat upright on the edge of a chair, aligned my head with my spine, centered my shoulders over my hips, and planted my feet firmly on the floor.

Sitting on the chair helped the strain in my back caused by the weight of my belly. The benefit for the warm-up was that I was able to breathe more fully while being supported by the seat of the chair.

4. Shortness of Breath

As a pregnancy goes along, breathing can become more difficult, because the organs essentially get smushed upward in order to make room for the growing baby. This makes it harder for the ribs to expand when you take in a breath, and harder for the diaphragm and abdominals to do their part in the breathing. During the last weeks of my pregnancy, I often found I had to take more sips of air and that I ran out of air more quickly as a result. To help free those muscles, I gently stretched the sides, front, and back of my rib cage before beginning the warm-up.

5. Support Muscles

The diaphragm and abdominals, often called the support muscles, are very important when using your voice and breathing. You may discover that these muscles tire more easily now that you are pregnant; however, you may also discover, as I did, just how much these muscles do work, for whenever I spoke or laughed, that growing belly moved a great deal.

Ultimately, this use of the abdominal muscles is a healthy thing during pregnancy. Gaining abdominal strength to support the weight of the baby in your belly will help you carry the baby, and it is suggested by some maternal fitness programs that it aids during delivery. I was advised against doing crunches to strengthen my abdominals while I was pregnant, so instead I took a maternal fitness class, which taught specialized abdominal exercises to engage the tummy muscles. Invariably, I found these exercises very beneficial for voice work.

Finally I want to say that, if you are pregnant, you should honor what your body is telling you from day to day as you practice the warm-up. And remember that these modifications are temporary.

PERSONAL REFLECTIONS ON THE VOCAL WORKOUT DURING PREGNANCY
By Katie Bull

During my first pregnancy, I had experienced an early complication and was told by my obstetrician/gynecologist to go on semi–bed rest and avoid vigorous exercise. So when there was no longer any risk, I was ready to *move*! Prenatal strengthening, stretching, and relaxation exercises were great for me at that time, because I needed to strengthen my abdominals in order to support my spine and relieve the pressure on my lower back, regain some aerobic fitness, and find stretching postures that were safe for me and the baby.

I needed to come out of the world of "pregnancy as illness." I needed to reclaim motion and trust what my body was telling me.

Pregnancy is such a profound and gentle cohabitation of spirits that I wanted to give my baby and myself whatever we needed to have the fullness of the experience. During the process of reclaiming my pregnant body and feeling its power, the vocal work was primary. The exercises were modified so that I would bounce only gently, and any twisting I did was always under the supervision of a registered nurse. As the pregnancy progressed, I found that the relaxation and strengthening work I had done was totally compatible with the relaxation exercises, breath work, and strengthening I was doing for my alignment and voice.

Indeed, the vocal exercises can and should be done during pregnancy, although, as the pregnancy progresses, they may need to be modified and adapted, depending on how you are carrying or whether you are at risk. Talk with your doctor or midwife and describe the more vigorous sections of the work. Even better: Show them the exercises.

During my two natural childbirths, I was able to draw on both instinct and practiced skills. My endurance was profound, and the births benefited from vocal practice. The vocal channel, as I discovered, is part of the birth channel. Birth energy is creative energy in its most elemental form.

For me, the balance of support, endurance, and release necessary during birth felt drawn from the same source as that which connects to, supports, and lets out sound. Breathing and relaxation are central in all birth practices. That I had done the vocal exercises during pregnancy supported my connection to my breath during the birth. During the rests between contractions, I was also able to draw from the "let go" mantra in the voice work. Because of the role of awareness in our vocal process, I was attuned to the laryngeal, thoracic, and perineal connection during birth—how the muscles of the throat and perineal region are neuromuscularly connected to the motion of the abdominal diaphragm. When the time came, I wasn't afraid of the power I needed to access in order to push and I wasn't inhibited about making sound. Let the birth be heard!

As I observe acting over the years, I am more and more inclined to believe that actors are born, not taught, and that a major reason for success is the God-given endowment of their physical apparatus. A unique voice can, perhaps, be a product of booze or testosterone or damaged vocal cords, but it can also be the product of exercise and experience and, most of all, of giving projection a place of prime importance in the actor's bag of tricks. With the advance of mechanical amplification, voices such as those of Ethel Barrymore, Katharine Cornell, and Eva Le Gallienne, Fredric March, Florence Reed, Alfred Lunt and Lynn Fontanne, and many more, have disappeared from the stage. Indeed, there has been a proportionate loss in the number of star actors, for voice is a major reason—voice and vitality, which is a part of voice—that any actor, any talent, becomes a star.

—Joe Stockdale

5

LEARNING FROM THE PAST:
John Barrymore and His Voice Teacher

It may surprise you to learn that actors have been studying and developing their voices since the ancient Greeks performed in Athens, more than two thousand years ago. Over the centuries, actors have had to speak using masks, or in huge outdoor theaters, or as in Shakespeare's day, in theaters where audiences were as interested in talking to each other as in listening to the play. Making your voice heard runs like a thread through the history of acting and actor training.

There is much that we can learn today from the actors of yesterday. Many of them brought a spirit of risk-taking to their vocal work. Many were discovering the relationship between voice and inner life for the first time. I have singled out the experience of the legendary American actor John Barrymore and his vocal coach Margaret Carrington, with whom he worked on productions of *Richard III* and *Hamlet* during the 1920s. At the time, Barrymore was considered a huge star—but not a classical actor. Determined to prove to himself and his public that he could act Shakespeare with the best of them, Barrymore worked with Carrington to alter both his voice and his performance style. It is a story of an actor's transformation, and through it I have learned a great deal about the tenacity and dedication required to achieve excellence on the stage.

Margaret Huston Carrington was born in 1877 near Toronto. From the time she was a youngster she had been a talented singer, and in 1896 she went to Europe, where she studied with the opera divas Emma Calvé and Nellie Melba. But at the height of her recital career, an accident permanently injured her vocal cords (she choked on a fishbone). After World War I began in 1914, she moved to New York and became a vocal coach for opera singers and actors, including her younger brother, Walter. Indeed, Walter Huston, who would one day become a stage and film star, always credited his sister with teaching him how to act.

Carrington was a commanding presence. She had red-gold hair and blue eyes that could stare a pupil into compliance. "You must be more obedient," she once told the actor and director Day Tuttle, after he arrived for a session at her Park Avenue apartment:

Stand at the end of the room . . . And do it again . . . And take your time. Nobody is hurrying you. Deepen your voice. Remember to breathe through the vowels, elongating them with downward inflections. Eventually we are going to find your basic sound, the basic sound you have never spoken, the sound that is Day Tuttle.

Charging no fee, and taking only the students who intrigued her—Barrymore, Orson Welles, Alfred Lunt (with the exception of Lillian Gish, she hardly ever taught women)—she helped them improve their breathing, enunciation, and the placement of their voice. She was not interested in what she called "vocal gymnastics," but in giving an actor the power to express feeling through a "personal sound." According to the scenic and costume designer Robert Edmond Jones, whom Carrington married after her first husband died, "She had come to believe that it was possible to free the speaking voice to such an extent that one could hear, not the speaker's intention or his personality, but his inner essence, the self, the soul, speaking through him."

Certainly John Barrymore needed Carrington's skill, intuition, and discipline.

Descended from a line of illustrious English and American actors, and the youngest of a theatrical trio that included his sister Ethel and brother Lionel, John Barrymore was the epitome of the matinee idol: Talented, handsome, and dissolute. At times more committed to womanizing and drinking than acting, he had made a career of playing light, undemanding comedies. Then in 1916, in John Galsworthy's *Justice*, he surprised critics with his touching, honest portrayal of a simple clerk who sacrifices himself to save the woman he loves from her brutal husband. Other performances in serious dramas followed, acted truthfully, without his previous artifice, and in 1920, the director and producer Arthur Hopkins asked Barrymore to play the villainous hero of Shakespeare's *Richard III*.

But the voice was not up to the task. Theater reviews testify that Barrymore's voice was definitely not his strongest asset. His enunciation was lazy, his projection poor. Critics complained that he sounded "dry" and monotonous. Audiences had difficulty hearing him.

"Jack had all the beauties except voice," said Hopkins. "There was a rasp which one feared could only be removed by a surgical miracle." Barrymore's uncle, the actor John Drew, put it more bluntly: "Jack speaks like a ruffian from Avenue A," he said.

The star agreed. He recalled that, shortly after he decided to attempt Richard III, "I went out into the woods . . . and recited the entire play, and then threw the book away. It couldn't be done. My voice had a high, nasal tone and I recited 'A horse, a horse, my kingdom for a horse!' like a terrified tenor trying to escape from a couple of blondes."

Six weeks before the production was scheduled to open, he went to Margaret Carrington for help.

In an essay called "The John Barrymore I Knew," written in 1942 (the year that both Carrington and Barrymore died), the voice teacher described the worried actor who had come to her home in 1920. He was, she recalled, "tremulous, modest and extremely shy"; he told her he was going to act Shakespeare and "was afraid of it."

"I could not believe that the most popular actor in America could be afraid of anything," Carrington wrote. "Then with the devastating Barrymore charm, he made me understand that he was asking me to help him."

She hesitated to take the project on. After all, they had only six weeks to work—not much time to undo the vocal problems Barrymore had spent thirty-eight years acquiring. "His voice was tired," she observed, "and in spite of its rare individual quality was of short range due to a complete lack of breath control."

But Barrymore's openness to her ideas convinced her that they could work together. "I had hoped to meet someone who would be receptive and responsive to one or two simple principles underlying speech control" Carrington wrote. "After my first hour with Barrymore, I knew that here was an actor who was simple and obedient enough to understand what these principles would do."

And so the matinee idol became Margaret Carrington's pupil.

It was not easy. Barrymore often took his lessons at Carrington's estate in Connecticut, and as Hopkins described it, when she became "exasperated by his vocal abominations, she frequently banished him to the garden to contemplate the violations." Still, Hopkins observed a chemistry between teacher and student that fulfilled both their needs:

Mrs. Carrington had the kind of derision that Jack appreciated. He took her most merciless barbs and went back for more. To her, he was the great opportunity that she long had sought. Just to find one voice that was really worth freeing, to hear just once the grandeur of Shakespeare's lines with unobstructed accompaniment. So, after long perseverance, two dreams were realized—Mrs. Carrington's and Jack's.

How does a teacher retrieve a voice that has suffered from decades of neglect? According to the actor Anthony Quinn, in whom Barrymore once confided about his experience, Carrington began by asking him simply to pick up an apple from a bowl on her table:

"Mr. Barrymore, what do you have in your hand?"
"I got a red apple."
"You have what?"
"I got a red apple."
"I'm sorry, I don't understand."
"You don't understand? I got a red apple in my hand."

Barrymore told Quinn that his lessons for the first two or three weeks were about making that apple sound like the juiciest, reddest apple in the world. She was working on allowing the sounds of the words to influence and contribute to the intellectual content of the text. "She taught me to make love to the words," he told Quinn.

Carrington was working on all areas of vocal expression from the start of their collaboration. She dealt with making his breathing more effective, and increasing the range and power of all the resonating areas, thus strengthening his voice. She taught him how to develop his vocal freedom, improve his articulation, and understand and effectively use the meter of the language.

He was extremely diligent. He would practice vowel sounds as he walked along the street, "prolonging them," wrote Carrington, "until he acquired the muscular control required to read through to the end of a sentence on one breath."

An infallible rule in reading Shakespeare is that it must be read to the punctuation set down in the texts. I do not know whether these punctuations [were] in Shakespeare's original manuscripts. In any case we cannot do better than to follow . . . the accredited editions in use today. We must read through the commas to the semicolons, which are suspended breath-pauses. It is only after the full stops that we can take a full breath. To do this demands the same breath support that singers and players of wind instruments must have when they phrase music. Actors who lack this power to breathe to the punctuations. . . break the continuity of the sense as well as the rhythm of the verse.

Certainly one aim was for Barrymore to sustain a line of Shakespearean verse. But Carrington wanted to do more than strengthen Barrymore's breath control. "The essence of the actor's craft," she wrote, "is to reveal the exact meaning of the text and at the same time to project the emotional content of the drama through his own personal sound."

Toward that end, she conveyed to Barrymore her approach to acting Shakespearean asides and soliloquies, with exciting results:

It might be defined as the difference between talking and thinking. The soliloquy must have only the sound of thought while dialogue is straightforward speech. But the real difficulty is that the audience is in on the soliloquy. How to bridge this seeming inconsistency depends on the actor's ability to project these two dimensions in sound. After [Richard's] scene with Lady Anne whom he cajoles and finally conquers . . . he is left alone on the stage, and has to say— "Was ever woman in this humor wooed? Was ever woman in this humor won?" To say the lines to himself lets the scene down. I suggested that he throw the speech right into the auditorium. The effect was startling . . . It took bold courage to step aside from tradition, and only an actor with Barrymore's natural theatre instincts could dare do it successfully.

Under her guidance, and with his talent and will, they forged a performance that merged realism and theatricality. "It is a superhuman test of an actor's ability to play a villain like Richard and project the beauty and significance of Shakespeare's text," Carrington wrote.

Richard's lines in the first scene give us a complete key to his character: "I that am curtailed by fair proportion . . . deformed, unfinished . . ." There is more in this speech than mere villainy. It is perhaps the greatest written revelation of human frustration . . . . Barrymore's entrance with a hump on his back and a limp was a startling apparition. . . . He was the living incarnation of Shakespeare's Richard.

By opening night, Hopkins was amazed at the change in Barrymore. "Mrs. Margaret Carrington," he said, "by some magic, entirely her own, had turned his faulty instrument into a medium of ease and beauty."

Richard III opened on March 6, 1920, at New York's Plymouth Theatre. Barrymore's performance was audacious. Here was a portrait that challenged tradition, acting which was purposefully low-key, and verse spoken clearly and purely. Instead of the physically powerful, emotionally turbulent Richard to which audiences were accustomed, Barrymore presented what one critic described as the "intellectual, stealthy, crafty and subtly malevolent royal monster." Barrymore had gone inside the character.

For the first time, critics praised the star's vocal quality, his range and control, and his diction. Francis Hackett in the *New Republic* was delighted: The actor's nasality had disappeared; his voice was now "beautifully placed, deep and sonorous and free." Alexander Woolcott in the *New York Times* announced that Barrymore "has acquired, out of space, a voice . . . rich, full and flexible. This is really the advance of which he may be proudest."

The role of Richard III became a benchmark in Barrymore's career. But it had come at a cost. After only thirty-one performances, Barrymore suffered a nervous breakdown, due maybe in part to his intense preparation. A year and a half later, when Barrymore and Hopkins spoke with Carrington about coaching the actor for *Hamlet*, Carrington agreed only on the condition that she and Barrymore have at least a month to work together before rehearsals began and that the production's opening date be set when she alone felt her student was ready.

In June 1922, Barrymore moved to Carrington's Connecticut farm and there he remained for two-and-a-half months. "What a happy summer that was," the teacher remembered. "We worked six, eight hours a day—sometimes into the night. In the garden—and the woods. The day he arrived, he was carrying an armful of books. . . I suggested that we put the books away and find out for ourselves what the play was about."

Carrington and Barrymore treated *Hamlet* as if it were a new play being performed for the first time, a psychological tactic on Carrington's part as much as an artistic one. "I think," she later concluded, "this accounted for his spontaneous . . . acting . . . and helped to banish any natural fear he might have had in appearing for the first time in a part that has been the high spot of every actor's experience."

She urged him not to memorize the part until they had explored every "shade of meaning," an approach that must also have contributed to Barrymore's spontaneity onstage. Asked frequently in later years why she and Barrymore spent so much time studying the script, she would explain that "Barrymore is the only actor I have ever known in America who was willing to polish every phrase of a play until he was satisfied that the deepest meaning of Shakespeare's texts [was] completely revealed and understood . . ."

Much of the polishing was at Carrington's insistence. When the voice teacher and her student retreated to the house, Carrington's niece, Margaret Walters, would often listen to the sessions from the next room. "He wasn't an easy pupil," she reported. "He had to be made to do things. I could hear her saying, 'Oh, no, no, no, no, no, Jack. Not like that—like this.' And she'd show him how. She'd say, 'Now I want you to breathe. And I want you to give that full value.'" She could often be overheard urging Barrymore to "Make it more relaxed" and avoid being "pompous."

If his performance of Richard III had revealed a new Barrymore, his portrayal of Hamlet in 1922, at the age of forty, permanently elevated Barrymore to the status of Shakespearean actor.

"Somebody ought to write a tale about Barrymore called 'The Story of a Voice,'" exclaimed the critic Heywood Broun in the *New York World*.

It is one of the most amazing adventures in our theatre. Here was a peculiarly pinched utterance distinctly marred by slipshod diction. Today it is among the finest voices in the American theatre. We don't mean that it vibrates and rumbles and roars, but that isn't our notion of a fine voice. It is attuned to talking. Hamlet never deafens the members of his family, the audience, or even himself.

Even Stark Young, the grudging critic for the *New Republic*, acknowledged that Barrymore "Has a beautiful presence, a profound magnetism, an English diction that is pure, even and exact, though not yet wholly flexible, and a voice which, though not supreme, is capable of the highest training and already in the middle part is very admirable."

The critics disagreed about how well Barrymore spoke the verse. Maida Castellun, apparently wed to an older performance style, wrote in the *New York Call* that the "splendors of passions and the soaring organ tones of Elizabethan rhetoric" were sadly absent from Barrymore's "colloquial, casual" performance.

But most reviewers praised Barrymore just because he dispensed with "soaring organ tones" and an overblown delivery. They liked his direct, natural style. Broun took to the conversational manner, and John Corbin in the *New York Times* noted that "the beauty of the rhythm was never lost."

Barrymore soon left the theater—and Shakespeare—for films. But shortly before his death, he told the actress Dorothy Gish that he was indebted to Margaret Carrington for his theatrical success, that without her he would have been "a fifth-rate actor."

Carrington's sessions with Barrymore continued during the *Hamlet* run. Playing such a large and strenuous role eight times a week for 101 performances—one more than the renowned Edwin Booth—was grueling vocally (also, Barrymore was not about to give up smoking). So Sundays would find the star working with Carrington to get his voice in shape for Monday.

When Barrymore took *Hamlet* to London in 1925, he asked Carrington to go, too. Distressed that many of the cast spoke

Shakespearean verse in a singsong manner, he wanted Carrington to help modernize their acting, the way she had adjusted his. The English actor E. Harcourt Williams remembered Carrington asking him, "'Why do you assume that particular voice when you are speaking Shakespeare? Do you do anything else besides Shakespeare?' I replied that I sometimes told stories to children. 'Tell me one then.' And I began, thoroughly amazed, to tell her Hans Andersen's "Tinder Box." 'But that's your real voice,' she exclaimed. 'That's the voice you ought to use in Shakespeare.' A flash of lightning could hardly have shown me more."

Years after Carrington coached Barrymore, she wrote about his presence and his acting:

No one ever saw him 'walk' on. He came in on the air. The only conclusion one can come to about these great personalities of the theatre and opera is that they were born possessed of a dynamo energy, to startle, to remind us that there is a power in certain people which defies analysis . . . Working with John Barrymore was like playing on a harp with a thousand strings.

I have come to recognize over the years of teaching acting that, many times, actors of college age experience rely on a "placed" or "idea" voice that is not their personal voice, and so the inner content of the text is not connected to the person talking. Instead, tension to "present" the meaning overtakes the acting, breathing is restricted, and no spontaneous vocal or physical life can happen. (Sometimes only personal emotions overtake the actor, and the vocal life is again restricted, and the audience remains unaffected emotionally.) The personal voice of an actor needs exploration.

—Joan Potter

6

HONESTY

I once heard Vanessa Redgrave say that observing the skill of American actors in playing psychological realism profoundly altered her view of acting. She was speaking of the American plays she had first seen in the 1950s. Most acting teachers, directors, and audiences would concur that Redgrave was referring to a quality of emotional honesty that she found in American acting. They would agree, too, that this is a desirable quality. Yet most would be hard-put to define what they mean by it. In terms of acting we might say that honesty is believability. In terms of vocal quality, what constitutes an honest voice? A sincere voice? A truthful voice?

An honest voice is one that connects the actor to his or her inner life, and thus responds to what the actor is feeling. You must trust that your instrument will be able to do this, for the honest voice is one that is never consciously manipulated to make the audience feel a particular way. You must also trust that your audience will understand that emotion.

DEVELOPING VOCAL HONESTY

Many actors equate honesty with quietness. They think the less volume and inflection they give their speeches, the more profoundly honest they will sound. Many British actors are being hired for big film roles because American directors associate their exceptional, transparent performances with quietness, a hallmark of the British style. In fact, more goes on in their performances than mere quietness. Quiet is quiet, loud is loud, and monotone is monotone. All may be honest or not.

Honesty stems from openness—a revealing, uncontrived vocal quality that allows the audience to read the actor's mind and heart. American actors consider themselves emotionally honest if they avoid vocally "illustrating" and vocally "indicating" their emotions. However, the lack of the negative value does not automatically supply the positive. No matter how freely and sincerely you feel an emotion, if your physical instrument is weak your emotion will be weakly transmitted to the audience.

The vocal flexibility and strength that you will develop through training will contribute to an honest vocal quality. But there is more: Many actors realize that an important component of giving a fresh, interesting performance involves *listening* to the other actors. Even so, few realize that listening also has a profound impact on the sound of their voices. An actor whose voice sounds phony or self-conscious probably will not be listening to the other actors. An actor who seems to calculate pauses is probably not listening to the other actors. Similarly, an actor who speaks too loudly or too softly is not listening, for excessive loudness is distancing to fellow actors and to the audience, and excessive softness suggests that you don't care whether the other actors or the audience hear you or not. On the other hand, an actor who really takes in what the other actors are saying is much more likely to be genuinely responsive.

Predetermining inflection on a particular line also tends to lead to dishonesty, and listening well is a good way to get past any preconceived ideas of how your character is supposed to sound. Your goal is to listen genuinely to the expression in the other actor's voice when he or she speaks, and for you to possess a vocal instrument which can express any emotion you feel as a result.

All the voice-training exercises in this book are designed to help you develop an honest voice (I'm using that term to mean a voice developed and efficient at communication) and they require paying attention to resonance, breathing, and unnecessary physical tension in the body. Unfortunately, some actors striving for naturalness in their portrayals find this work interfering. But the conflict they suppose they will find between voice work and emotional work is not real. There is no conflict. Working on having a more responsive, open, and developed vocal instrument can really make your emotional inner life more present. Your inner life will be expressed with more clarity and intensity. In order to accomplish this integration, it is vital to do the voice exercises with awareness of what you are feeling.

This does not necessarily mean you must experience profound emotion as you carry out vocal exercises, but you must feel a connection to whatever you are experiencing at the moment. As you will discover, voice exercises practiced in this manner lead to honesty in acting.

QUESTIONS OF APPROACH

One way or another, voice training has always been part of the actor's job. As an actor, you must be very clever regarding training, ruthlessly deciding if particular instruction adds to or interferes with your performances. And as I hope to show, not only the type of voice training you receive is very important, but also the timing—the point at which training is incorporated into your acting process—is crucial.

Of the many different approaches to training the actor's voice, one fairly common one still being used by some teachers is *optimal pitch.* With this approach, the teacher determines the area within the range of the actor's voice that is best heard, and the actor learns to "place" his or her voice in that area. The problem with this method is that it does not take into account what is being expressed. For example, if your character is calming down a hysterical child, you will want to call on the lower, relaxed part of your voice. On the other hand, if your character wants to yell, "Help!" as someone approaches with a butcher knife, you will need a vibrant, aggressive, higher part of your voice. That is, the yell should happen naturally, and not be "placed" or controlled. With the optimal pitch method you will have to struggle to produce these different emotions from the same spot in your vocal range. In fact, it will be impossible. To be at your best, your entire vocal range must be available to you.

It is instructive to consider an actor who was caught without a voice that could serve him in his role: Marlon Brando as Mark Antony in the 1953 film of Shakespeare's *Julius Caesar*. Brando was a wonderful actor, but his vocal instrument was underdeveloped; as a result he could not convey all of the character's internal passion. A better instrument would have made Brando even more effective and, in this case, more honest.

Part of the American actor's tendency to be suspicious of voice training derives from the way we perceive our national character. Early in our history, we learned to judge people by their deeds rather than their words. American mythology emphasizes the nobility of strong, silent men and women who adhere to a code of honesty and act from inner conviction.

We admire people who live full emotional lives with considerable sensitivity, yet outwardly express little. We are, after all, a nation of doers. When you translate the American character into an acting style (especially in the movies), you wind up with a lean, spare performance seething with underlying emotion. The audience empathizes with the actor and imagines what he or she is feeling. Good American film actors, such as Gary Cooper, have shown a remarkable ability to think and feel their roles while showing almost nothing vocally. Observations have been made time and again that if you watch good actors working in front of a camera, you can't see them doing anything. But when you see the same performance on the screen, the whole character is visible.

The English tradition more actively encourages voice development than the American. The English also have a centuries-old history of valuing the spoken word and, as a natural consequence, the voice itself. Ironically, the English sometimes work in an understated style better than we do. Alec Guinness's BBC-television portrayal of the detective George Smiley is a masterpiece of restrained playing. Anthony Hopkins's completely held-back portrayal of the butler in the film *The Remains of the Day* boils with emotion.

In acting, holding back can, and often does, create intensity. However, we get into trouble when this leads to undervaluing the physical instrument and overvaluing the inner emotional life. Even if you take the position that emotional life is the essence of acting, the emotion must still be effectively expressed. The stronger and richer your emotional life is, the greater your need for a superior method of release.

What we're talking about here is finding an approach that enables the actor to work at full power, using all of his or her gifts in a smoothly integrated performance. When I first started teaching in conservatory programs, voice, speech, and movement were treated as though they were separate from acting. It was assumed that training the vocal and physical instrument would somehow carry over into acting. In my first year of teaching voice in a prominent B.F.A. program, I was shocked to learn that final scenes, performed in front of a jury of faculty members, were judged for acting alone; voice and speech were judged by poetic recitations (movement was not judged at all). The faculty's view was that voices cannot be judged in the context of scenes. In their approach, no effort was made to help actors integrate voice, speech, and movement into scene work. On the contrary, much effort was spent in continuing to separate scene work from voice, speech, and movement. These acting teachers expected their students to use only the specific techniques being taught in their particular acting classes, without any integration of other skills and knowledge.

All actor-training teachers, regardless of their specialties, need to help actors integrate their skills. When skills are not integrated, performances are less than they should be. What's more, actors often wind up with vocal and acting problems.

HEIGHTENED AWARENESS

A myth is often promoted about acting: It is frequently said that when an actor is acting well, he is so "honest" he isn't even aware that he is onstage or before the camera. That is plain silly. The truth is that to act well you must be in a state of heightened awareness.

Onstage, in addition to your body and voice, you must deal with the set and the blocking and also be aware sometimes of the stage manager and the audience. If you find the chair you're supposed to sit upon in the wrong place, you must adjust and move it or depart from the original blocking. (Hopefully, you would not pretend that nothing is wrong and sit where the chair isn't!) You must be super-aware, not less aware. Artists do not work in vacuums. Art—any kind of art—involves the conscious use of *craft*.

I do an exercise with my students to underscore this point. We rehearse a scene, and then I send them away and ask them to prepare themselves to perform the scene. While they're gone, I drastically change the set. I turn the furnishings around. I remove some of the chairs, turn some of them upside down, and I move others to different parts of the stage. When the actors return, I tell them to begin. They move the chairs and do whatever they need to do to get the scene underway. Invariably, they adjust. An actor must deal with everything—all of it, all the time.

"Awareness" need not mean concern or worry. For example, if you feel your voice tightening up or going "into your throat," you should be aware of that but also know what to do about it, even as you go on acting. This is the sign of a skilled professional who is aware of his or her instrument. As you do the vocal workout described in this book, you will begin to feel your voice vibrating in your body; you will become aware of your voice both when you are acting and when you are simply going about the business of everyday life. You don't actually listen to yourself (a sure way to be a bad actor), but you do develop an awareness of how your instrument is working, which will allow you to make any necessary adjustments even in the midst of a performance.

TRAINING THE VOICE DURING ACTOR TRAINING

I once worked with an acting teacher in a conservatory program who had spray-painted this message on the studio wall: "The Words Come Last." I know what he was driving at: Don't just repeat the words mindlessly; they must have the force of emotion behind them, they must be said by a person (or a character). However, his memorable phrase is simplistic and unworkable. What the actor ends up remembering is: "Words Don't Count," and consequently, voice and speech skills don't really count. (One respected colleague remarked to me, "What he really means is that the words never come at all.") It was interesting to me that when this and similar influences became prominent in this conservatory program, the school began graduating actors with very low levels of voice, speech, and movement skills—thus negating the point of conservatory training. If the focus on feeling means that words and voice are not dealt with, then the instrument is not being adequately addressed, and the actor is not being encouraged to do consistent work on developing his or her voice.

Virtually all American actor-training is now based on actors using their own emotional lives, so that an actor can be true, real, in the moment, and fresh in a part each time he or she performs it. But how and when does voice training fit into this approach? Many actors unfortunately work hard to get in touch with their emotional lives, but start thinking about developing the vocal instrument afterward. That's like studying the emotional content of a concerto and then learning to play the piano, or exploring the emotional life of the role of Giselle and then learning to dance. Voice training that is tacked on to the end of actor training will never be successfully integrated into performance.

Worse, the tacked-on approach can interfere with your ability to give an honest performance. Consider the actor who spends weeks finding Hamlet's inner emotional life, a process for which he doesn't use much vocal energy. When he tries to act that Hamlet, much of his work will not carry. He is now faced with an impossible situation: If a voice coach comes in and works with him on breathing and vocal release at the end of the rehearsal process, his truth can and often does disappear. John Barrymore worked on his voice before and during the rehearsals of *Richard III* and *Hamlet*—not as an afterthought. The great actress Lynn Fontanne explained it this way: "If you act it quietly and naturally in a small room and it sounds beautiful to you and then you go on the stage and have to project, it all seems destroyed."

Many actors know this and use it as a reason to reject voice work. Fontanne's own solution was to work with constant energy and vitality, to "act it up—fully" from the beginning, even when experimenting in early rehearsals. In that way, she said, when inner truth was realized, the voice and energy were already integrated.

With the same goal in mind, voice training takes a somewhat different approach. My belief is that voice training should come before, or at the same time as, emotional and other acting work (motivation, character, and so on), and in equal measure. In this way the vocal instrument will be operating fully from the beginning, so that any attention to voice can contribute to, rather than detract from, the actor's effort to develop a character's internal life and express that work onstage.

The very heart of acting is embedded in the word, the language. The thought is projected into the world through the act of producing vibration. If the voice is not developed, expanded, full, and flexible enough to fill these words, particularly in heightened language, the meaning and the action are lost, and the audience cannot understand what is being said. They may hear, but they do not grasp the intentions, because the actor is not being expressive and does not possess the technical vocal ability to go beyond his or her own rhythms and vocal habits. This is very much an issue that is peculiar to the United States, where voice work and language are not emphasized. Voice work is not an ingrained part of the American acting tradition, as it is, for instance, in England.

As a voice teacher and acting teacher with origins that are other than American, I do not make a distinction between the two disciplines. I teach acting through the voice, through language, because the acting impulse is in the breath, the action is in the word, and the channel for bringing it to life is the human voice. I have Chuck to thank for this understanding. His approach, the way in which he teaches the actor to be in the moment of the breath, to listen to the breath, to develop a physical awareness rather than manipulate muscles and listen to the sound they are making, all contributed to my becoming a better actor. I have filtered this work through my own sensibility and responses, through the feedback I receive from my students, and though my own process as an actor. As do all of us, when we learn from our great mentors and continue to pass on the "good news."

—Judylee Vivier

7

BEING HEARD

The bottom line is that unless you are playing someone who doesn't talk, you have to be heard, one way or another. There are so many misconceptions about this issue and so many misunderstandings and disagreements that the subject becomes difficult sometimes to deal with. Even though most theatrical mediums use some form of amplification these days, every actor needs to be able to work without a microphone. Any actor who has a great deal of experience takes this for granted. Until the advent of rock musicals in the late 1960s, when amplification suddenly took over the theater, stage actors assumed that their job was to be absolutely real *and* be heard in the theater, including in the last row of the balcony. Today, many young actors mistakenly believe that they must choose between being real and being heard.

If you are working without amplification, being heard is up to you. Of course, theaters may have good, poor, or so-so acoustics. Thus the assumption that any talented actor should be audible in any theater, expressing any kind of emotion, from the most intimate to the most powerful, is illogical and wrong. If you must speak very, very loudly in order to be heard, your acting will change; your performance cannot be the same as it is when you are speaking intimately in a rehearsal hall. Some actors have trouble accepting this fact, because they have been told they should be able to make a loud sound and be intimate at the same time. They cannot, and it is critical to accept this.

If you are rehearsing a tender love scene in a small rehearsal studio and then move to a larger theater space, you will not be heard unless you speak up, and then, automatically, your expression will become less intimate. In this situation, you will have to make a decision, for you cannot just raise the volume and pretend that you are delivering the same performance you discovered in rehearsal—it's physically impossible. You will have to sacrifice, or change, something, and your own aesthetics will enter into the choice you make. In this circumstance, some actors prefer a strong voice, no matter what emotion they express. Others dislike the bigger presentation and always, no matter what is expressed, underplay the vocal energy. And still others prefer a more old-fashioned theatrical voice that stands out. Of course, if you have a very developed and efficient vocal instrument, it will be much easier for you to be heard and will take much less effort, no matter which choice you make.

But remember that most people do not go to the theater or the movies to hear a great voice. They go to experience a performance. (Some, of course, think a show is good only when they're hit over the head with sound, while others are willing to lean into the play and listen more closely.) As already suggested, you can develop a voice that allows you to be heard *and* that is also honest, personal, and revealing. Later we will discuss how developing *resonance* and other vocal qualities will help you do this. But first, consider three approaches to audibility that you're likely to encounter: Projection, pitching up, and amplification.

PROJECTING THE VOICE

Projecting is the old-fashioned solution to not being heard. We all use the term; it's pervasive in the theater. But bear with me here, because there are serious drawbacks to this concept. (And I'm not suggesting the alternative: Not being heard.)

Suggestions like "Throw your voice to the balcony" or "Remember the little old lady in the last row" disconnect the actor from inner emotion. Exertion—pushing the sound—separates the voice from the actor's internal emotional life. Indeed, the projected "stage voice" is usually too loud, too slow, and too impersonal. With an overemphasis on articulation, it usually includes an exaggerated, artificial speech pattern or rhythm. Because the actor's speech is manipulated into certain preplanned inflections, the stage voice becomes a distancing voice not at all useful for a contemporary actor. It is not honest, and certainly not what my voice work is all about. Speak the following line from Shakespeare's *Richard III* slowly, loudly, and with exaggerated speech (that is, with all the clichés of a "stage" voice):

Now is the winter of our discontent
Made glorious summer by this sun of York;

The lines probably will sound theatrical, but they cannot possibly sound honest. Such an approach does not serve the actor's artistry.

PITCHING UP

Pitching up is another solution that brings vocal exertion. The term means talking in a higher, less intimate, part of the voice. Usually, pitching up results in an impersonal performance; it sounds elevated and "actorish." Some audiences like this effect, but I find that it contributes to a less personal use of the voice and is very limited.

AMPLIFICATION

Some of the best American performers who emerged during the 1940s and '50s established an intimate, honest acting style—and they could also be heard. Actors like Maureen Stapleton, Jason

Robards, and Kim Stanley took it for granted that, onstage, they would be working without amplification, and so they made it their business to be audible.

Of course, the Broadway theaters they inherited were of medium size, and many possessed wonderful acoustics. Perhaps more importantly, audiences at the time listened differently than audiences do now. In fact, playwrights and directors often deliberately allowed for a short period at the beginning of each play to let the audience adjust to hearing the words. (You will notice this "stall" when you see an unedited revival of an older drama; there seems to be a slight lapse before the central action gets under way.)

These days, as noted earlier, all actors must deal with amplification of one kind or another at some point in their careers. No one makes a living only on small stages; you must be able to work in television and film, and many large theaters now rely on electronic wizardry to deliver the actors' voices to the audience. In the largest theaters, in spaces with impossible acoustics, and on most outdoor stages, amplification is probably essential.

In some cases, the existence of contemporary sound technology has actually prompted theater architects to design halls that accommodate large audiences. Actors are then equipped with body microphones—are "miked"—even if they have the vocal capacity to be heard in the last row of the balcony in a normal-sized theater.

In this situation, miking can be a limited friend to actors, for it prevents them from having to throw their voices into a great void. However, theater people often think that amplification can overcome *any* acoustical problem. This, of course, is a mistaken assumption.

In truth, amplification tends to flatten out the voice and make it less expressive. It also tends to distort the voice and separate the actor from the audience, largely because the sound emanates from a speaker that is positioned dozens of feet from the actor. There is something unnatural about seeing live actors open their mouths to speak, but hearing their voices come from somewhere else in the auditorium. What's more, the actors onstage can usually hear their displaced voices coming from the speakers, which is distracting for the actor and distancing for the audience.

The effect of amplification has gone even deeper: It has also changed audiences' experience of the theater. With the supposed help of modern amplification, an audience needn't concentrate on the actors and what they are saying. The sound is delivered to the audience, and the audience participates less actively in the theatrical event. There is a huge difference between an audience's energy going toward the stage in order to listen and an audience being hit over the head with sound from all around the auditorium.

I once had a student in Neil Simon's *Brighton Beach Memoirs* on Broadway. One night the sound system failed during the first act. The actors continued playing, and the audience became quieter and grew more involved in the play. The actors actually found themselves talking more honestly with each other. The next day, the actors asked management to leave the system off. Management refused. Amplification has become the norm.

In a workable theater with good acoustics, I still prefer the natural voice, although if everyone else was wearing a body mike, I doubt if I would say no—it would put me at a strange disadvantage. But as the director Joe Stockdale has said, "I've never heard an amplified voice convey the nuances of the human voice, any more than a microphone can enhance the sound of a Stradivarius."

WORKING IN FILM AND TELEVISION

The good actor wants to be honest onstage, in film—in every medium—which means his or her vocal approach has to be consistent from one medium to the other. But in the past twenty years I have worked with enough successful film and television actors to understand that they can have certain unique vocal problems, especially with amplification. One prominent film actor intentionally speaks so quietly that there is almost no vibration in his voice. I am told that he is trying to add intensity to his performance. His fellow actors often can't hear him in their scenes, which has a negative effect on their performances and his. In the sound mix, the engineer must turn up the volume on his lines so that the audience will hear him, and this creates an artificial effect, because the actors he is working with do not hear him during filming, and their performances are out of sync with his. The final result is a less engaging performance from all.

In film and television, as onstage, the microphone amplifies whatever is being expressed. If your voice lacks feeling, that lack will be amplified, and naturally any vocal problems or limitations you have will be amplified as well.

In regard to breathing, film actors may tell you that paying attention to it comes across as phony in sound recording. They are right—if they define breathing as a mechanism disconnected from their emotions and thoughts. However, as long as your breath is linked to your thought and motivation, paying attention to breathing helps your acting. This is particularly true when you are miked. When your breathing is connected to your inner life, you cannot sound phony.

You need to be aware of the advantages and limitations of being amplified. But to reach your full potential as an actor, you must be expressive, amplified or not.

DEVELOPING RESONANCE

The actor must have a well-developed vocal instrument that is able to produce sound with little physical effort. A *resonator* is an area where the voice becomes larger. The mask area of your face—the sinuses, nose, and cheeks—is a major resonating area. There, vibrations produce an *overtone* in your entire voice that allows the voice to be clear and carry more easily. American actors tend to underutilize this crucial area. But when the nose and cheek areas are insufficiently developed, the voice usually has a colloquial sound that seems unrefined. It works for some contemporary roles, but is inadequate for many others.

These sound vibrations are not to be confused with the sound you make by pitching up, for the overtone is present throughout most of your vocal range. It does not interfere with any expression or with the freedom of your vocal instrument. On the contrary, developing the overtone contributes to expression.

In situations where you are working without amplification, you are hopefully going to be in a relatively small or well designed theater. If your vocal instrument is well developed, you will probably not have to be concerned about speaking up or projecting. Just keep on doing what you're doing. The audience will lean in a little. If a director tells you to speak up, you can do that by releasing your voice a little more. By "releasing" I mean letting go, rather than pushing or using effort. It is like the difference between dropping an object (releasing it) and throwing it. It involves opening up or expanding, rather than pushing and compensating for a weakness. Releasing the voice is addressed in all the liberating exercises. Remember, when some people say, "I can't hear you," what they really mean is, "I can't understand you." There is a difference, and it's your job to figure it out.

You want to make sure your release is backed up by your acting. Your acting will be different when you speak louder, but it must remain honest. Sacrificing honesty in order to be heard is not an option.

None of this is simple. It involves taste, aesthetics, talent, skill, and the willingness to be interested and involved in developing your vocal instrument through intelligent and effective daily workouts.

The silencing of women has occurred in many ways, including making women self-conscious about the sound of their voices. Women often share with me the feeling that they don't sound "right." In their minds, there is an elusive sound of the idealized feminine, always just out of reach. But women should not have to fight the imposed degradation of being told that they sound too "emotional," "sexual," or "angry." Women need to allow themselves variety of tone and freedom of expression.

—Emily Caigan

8

CHARACTER
AND GENDER

THE VOICE IN CHARACTER WORK

Actors often ask me how to achieve a voice that differs from their own for a particular character role. Dustin Hoffman's voice changed, for instance, when he played Willy Loman in Arthur Miller's *Death of a Salesman* on Broadway. And if you think about it, Hoffman has adopted a variety of voices during his career. Still, somehow he always manages to connect them to his inner feelings.

But when teachers describe "character voice work," they often mean an external idea of a character's voice. In other words, they are suggesting you read the play and research your character, then decide intellectually what kind of voice you want to use for the part. But this is playing an idea of a voice. It is an intellectual decision, rather than a choice derived from an inner emotional experience. As such, it often rings false.

I believe that character work is the same as any other aspect of an acting assignment. When you create a character, you do not want to practice making a particular sound, but rather allow your voice to change in response to what you are experiencing and expressing. With few exceptions, the key to good character work is to develop a responsive vocal and physical instrument.

Think of playing Laura in *The Glass Menagerie*. You cannot play this very shy character by being shy yourself. You might think that Laura's voice should be very small. However, Laura's actions and words, as supplied by the dramatist, Tennessee Williams, fully describe the nature of her shyness. What, then, does the actor supply? If she has an expressive voice, she will be able to reveal Laura's inner life. When she talks about blue roses or her glass animals, she should be painfully vulnerable, but given the delicate symbolism of Laura's lines, it would be dangerous to play her using a tiny, weak voice. It makes more sense to use a fully expressive voice, to reveal her thoughts and feelings.

If your voice is responsive to the character's inner life, and you are playing a very depressed person, your voice will probably have little energy and perhaps be deeper. If you are playing a joyful person, your voice will respond to that emotion and reflect it. This will happen without manipulation, if your vocal instrument is open and the acting is honest. After all, human beings have particular voices because they possess certain emotional and physical realities. This being true in real life, it is also true of any character you play.

When you act a character part, think about allowing your voice to respond to the character's physical reality. For example, when playing a person much older than yourself, you need to deal with the physical aspects of aging. How does aging affect the spine, the breathing? How do those changes then affect the voice? Avoid playing a vocal cliché—a particular sound that you assume an older person would have. If you approach the character from a physical point of view, and your instrument responds to the changes you make in your own body, the result will be real.

As we have already established, you also want your voice to be affected by the character's emotional reality. Manipulating the voice to sound as if you are feeling something you do not really feel will scarcely ring true.

VOICE AND GENDER

Actors not only make the mistake of imposing their idea of a character's voice, they also limit their vocal ability by yielding to general cultural notions about male and female vocal traits. Society imposes vocal constraints on men and women. In our culture, for instance, women are encouraged to use facial-mask resonators (nasal passages, sinuses, and cheeks), which produce clarity and brilliance, in order to sound childlike and feminine. Men, on the other hand, are encouraged to use chest resonance, which produces vocal power. However, if you only use chest resonance, your voice remains flat. Each gender ends up being shortchanged, because each ends up using only half a vocal range—far too limiting for an actor.

By accepting the stereotypical idea of how a woman should speak, many women wind up with a breathy quality, a mixture of breath and vibration that produces a weak, childish sound. The voice often has both a manipulative and apologetic quality. Women who dare to develop chest resonance often worry that they will be accused of sounding phony and theatrical, or masculine. It is seldom the case that any of these is a real danger. Female actors who have made the choice to cultivate the full range of their voices have told me that other people react quite positively to the change, both in their work and their everyday lives. Other actors listening to them invariably say the female voice that includes chest resonance sounds sexy, womanly, rich, and honest, and the women themselves claim that they feel something change within themselves. When a woman's voice is stronger, she usually feels stronger.

I often receive inquiries from female business executives who tell me that their weak voices are limiting their careers. Indeed, in addition to daily conversations with colleagues, dozens of critical career-building situations draw attention to an individual's voice. These include making client presentations, chairing conferences, and giving speeches. Executives who want to advance their careers pursue these opportunities and try to make a strong impression. A highly visible executive working her way up in the fashion industry once told me, "I'm tired of being asked to put my mother on the phone, when the caller really wants to talk to me." Her voice sounded childlike rather than mature.

Just as the voice can reflect a cultural stereotype, it can also be a factor in type casting. Actresses frequently tell me, "I don't want to be limited to playing ingénues or kooky parts." Men tell me they are expected to sound strong and invulnerable, as if they felt no emotion. Encouraged as youngsters to use only the lower half of their voices, boys wind up with little freedom to reveal what they are feeling when they grow up. As a result, adult men avoid using the upper part of their voice range and, specifically, their nasal resonators. Because these habits are culturally ingrained, it is no surprise that male actors in America are often caught in this trap.

One very successful, intense, captivating young actor whom I have observed has the habit of restricting his voice to his chest tones. I assume he does this deliberately, because using only the lower part of his vocal range gives his voice a distinctive, almost choking sound, and gives his acting a quality of tightly controlled rage. When he loses that control in a scene, the contrast between held-in fury and suddenly released anger is explosive to watch.

The downside of his particular technique is that much of the time the listener can't understand what he is saying, because the sound is buried in his chest. If he were to incorporate facial-mask overtones into his range, his voice would have more clarity, without sacrificing the deep chest tones he uses to help connect himself to his emotions.

In my experience, male business executives have more trouble making vocal changes than male actors do. To many men, physical relaxation, which is needed to keep the voice flowing, feels like weakness, whereas tension feels strong and dynamic. But clearly, physical tension is not the same thing as strength, and it blocks vocal production. When I was teaching at the State University of New York at Purchase, I was often asked to work with executives from businesses in the area. Many of them were having serious vocal problems; often they lost their voices when they spoke in public. But letting go of tension and relaxing felt so weak to them, they found it difficult to understand the need for change.

Relaxation is neither feminine nor masculine. Men can certainly develop the ability to relax, which ultimately will make the voice stronger and more masculine, and definitely more expressive and interesting. In women, relaxation results in a warmer, richer sound. Men sometimes need to become more vulnerable, and women often need to become more powerful. Actors must possess all human qualities and be able to express them. It helps to understand the gender-based restrictions society has placed on you all your life and observe how these restrictions are manifested in your voice and body. Once you recognize the restrictions, you can make vocal changes.

The gender-based limitations extend to breathing. Unless they are trying to hold in their abdominal muscles for cosmetic reasons, men are allowed to be fairly free in their breathing. By contrast, women are encouraged to suck in the belly and breathe only in the chest. Although few women wear corsets these days, they are supposed to look as if they do. Holding in the belly all the time is a constriction that causes tension in the whole body. As Emily Caigan, a former student, has written:

> I began working with Chuck Jones in 1991, while I was an actress. He used to say, "Women no longer wear corsets, they're just supposed to sound and look as though they do." This one statement was the key to unlocking my activism. For the first time, I understood how my body and thoughts, and thus my spirit, had been influenced and controlled by society, politics, and standards of beauty. There were no longer boned encasements restricting my breath and voice production, but every time I held my stomach in so as not to look "fat," the result was the same.

Through Chuck's exercises, I learned to release my belly and my soft palate. The tension of tightening these muscles had forced my voice into a higher range than my released speaking voice naturally created. I no longer have this problem, and by using these exercises I have access to my full voice and I have changed my life. Now as a teacher, I am fortunate to witness this transformation in others.

One more story. An African-American man in my class regularly spoke with a high tone. I had heard the lower tones in his voice, but it was difficult for him to use them when he spoke; his body would tense up. Then one day I got it. I asked Tom a very direct question and hoped I wouldn't offend him. "Tom," I said, "do you feel like you have to be nice to people so that they're not intimidated by you?" He started to laugh, "Yah, all the time," he answered. Tom is well over six feet tall and has a strong build. I said, "I think that's why it's hard for you to use your chest resonance. What if you didn't have to take care of other people's reactions?" He was silent and then he said, "People cross the street when they see me coming." The next time he brought his monologue into class he used his full voice and was amazing. We all applauded him.

With the current popularity of aerobics classes, both men and women are walking around holding in their abdominal muscles. This almost guarantees a held-back and tight voice. In fact, I get many calls from aerobics teachers who have lost their voices, invariably a result of constant tension in the belly. These teachers simply do not get enough breath to support the level of vocal production needed for giving classes, and the results are damaged vocal cords and voice loss.

These teachers are overlooking a critical relaxation factor that could not only protect the voice but also enhance physical training. After all, when you do curls at the gym, you tense your biceps doing the exercise, but then you put the weights down and go on with your life—you don't hold your biceps in a contracted position all day. As far as your belly goes, you can do all the pulling-in (transverse) exercises and crunches and sit ups you want—just release them afterward. Look at the Greek statues of athletic men. Their muscled midsections are not held or pulled in. And most people would like to look that good. It seems hard for people to understand that there is no muscle which needs to be tensed or held all the time. We could afford to open up our thinking on this point.

To have a successful, long-lasting career, every actor, male and female, needs to develop the entire voice, bottom to top, and the capacity to be vulnerable and to be powerful. Your most moving moments as an actor will come when you drop societal constraints and show all the layers of your character's humanity. Do the vocal workout daily and explore all the areas of your voice, even those that feel awkward and foreign or wrong, masculine or feminine. Let your voice encompass all of it.

I believe vocal training is most effective when closely coordinated with training in acting and movement. An actor's goal is to become an integrated and flexible organism upon which each text can act, and through which each character can speak. When the voice is freed, it becomes a powerful channel for emotional and imaginative release, able to readily mirror a text.

—Linda deVries

9

VOCAL POWER

Vocal power is the ability to express strong emotions using the voice. Genuine vocal power is rare. The greatest test, I believe, is one's ability to express anger: If you can be vocally powerful when expressing anger, you usually can be vocally powerful during all emotional responses.

People avoid vocal power for several reasons. First, it can be frightening to take responsibility for what you say. Vocal power means you are really saying something—putting yourself on the line—and that takes courage. Also, because most of us have trained ourselves since childhood to be vocally subdued, developing vocal power becomes uncomfortable. Power itself feels dangerous and wrong. To rationalize their habit of holding back, actors point out, "It's more intense to hold back." Or they simply say, "Less is more." The truth is that sometimes less is less. Every performing artist needs the capacity to be powerful when power is called for. We all know how to hold back, if needed.

Vocally, power comes from vibration in one important resonating area of the body: The torso, or chest. You'll notice that when expressing anger many people allow their voices to go quite high in pitch, which sounds strained and—if you think about it—weak. Including chest resonance in the vocal range reduces that high squeak and produces vocal power. But adding chest resonance to your vocal range takes some getting used to. There is a distinct difference between lowering your pitch and utilizing chest resonance. The first sounds artificial and manipulated. Think about the wonderfully phony news-anchorman's voice that actor Ted Knight used on the television sitcom *The Mary Tyler Moore Show*. You could actually see Knight tuck his chin in, deliberately lower his pitch, and produce his Ted Baxter on-camera voice. His performance was brilliant. By contrast, using chest resonance correctly sounds genuine, free, and powerful; it's full vocally.

Producing vocal power is a matter of taking a full breath, letting go, and bringing your chest resonance into play along with all your other resonators. You want to use the amount of vibration needed to match the emotion—you don't want to produce too little or too much sound for the content. If you are instrumentally open, you will naturally get the right amount of sound.

Let's say you have a role in which you must express anger. Most actors will either push their voices or hold back. If you think you express anger best by pushing, your voice probably tightens, goes higher, and sounds strident. It's possible to damage your vocal cords that way. You may think the result sounds strong, but in fact, you are compensating for a constricted voice—forcing sound from a less vibratory instrument. Moreover—and this is important—to the audience your anger comes across as weakness, because audiences subconsciously pick up any residual feelings of inadequacy you have.

It's often hard to stop yourself from pushing, because the physical tension created by pushing can feel like anger, and when you stop pushing, you may feel you aren't expressing anything. But this is part of a strange phenomenon in acting: *When real emotion is released in the voice, the actor feels less of the emotion.* He or she is letting the emotion out.

Both pushing against tension and holding back can make the actor feel more emotion inside, but the audience receives less because the actor doesn't actually let the emotion out vocally. If the actor is inwardly full of emotion, the audience usually senses that something is going on within the actor, but doesn't perceive what that is. Thus, pushing or holding back never achieves the same result as actually releasing a powerful emotion.

Releasing or letting go of anger can be a real vocal challenge. For practice, I ask actors to speak a text rapidly, because there is automatically more release when you are talking fast. I did this for years before I read Laurence Olivier's *Confessions of an Actor*, in which he described how he used this technique to great effect. Try it now. Speak this angry line slowly: "Now get out of here."

Now . . . get . . . out . . . of . . . here!

Now repeat the same line very quickly. If you mean it both times, the slower delivery will be more controlled. The second version will be more released.

In real life, slow delivery protects the listener from your wrath. In acting, however, you don't always want to be protective; sometimes you want to sound dangerous and threatening, or at least be powerful by being honest and open.

Here is another series of exercises to increase your awareness of how you are using your voice. The lines you'll be saying are:

All right, I want to deal with this now. When I tell you to do a job, I mean do it this instant. Now!

I want you to act these lines three different ways:

1. Say the lines honestly, but hold back vocally, as if you didn't want someone to hear in another room. The expression is contained anger. This could be a valid choice, but I hope not your only one.

2. Push your voice slightly. That means, use more voice than you really need to express what you are communicating.

People do this all the time; however, it can sound phony (too much voice), and there is always the possibility of damaging your voice.

3. Now try releasing the lines. Be open, honest, and use a voice that truly expresses the right amount of anger—no less, no more. Use chest resonance, without going higher in pitch. This requires a full breath, connected to your desire to express your thoughts and emotions.

All three of these approaches are valid; just be careful with the pushing, because you can hurt your voice if you push too much. Remember again that pushing always communicates weakness. I can't say that enough. If that is your intention, then it may be all right as a choice. However, usually it is not an intelligent choice, because physically you put yourself in a vulnerable position.

And if you must express hysteria, possibly the most heightened emotional state you would ever have to express onstage, consider your own survival. As a professional, you must learn how to protect yourself, and with a developed instrument you will be able to be effective emotionally and vocally without hurting yourself. Vocal power is worth working toward because it helps the actor to liberate all emotions, and including power in your range allows you to be strong when you need to be. There is something to be said for subtlety, but there is a great deal to be said for giving a direct, open, powerful expression.

When I started working with Chuck to improve my voice, I had no idea that his work would fundamentally change my approach to my acting and all my creative work. Through the exercises, I reclaimed parts of myself that had been hidden by tension and fear. My deepest feelings emerged. As we worked on pieces of material in class, I was gradually able to express parts of my soul that had been shut away for years. My whole being, and especially my voice, were transformed. Working from the inside out and not the other way around—with a good vocal instrument—changed everything.

The process of reclaiming a complete sense of my self and integrating it into my voice and work was not always easy. During many weeks in class, I cried uncontrollably every time I read Stephen Spender's sonnet "I think continually of those who were truly great." It brought up overwhelming feelings of grief and confusion. Chuck's encouragement to stay with myself and the process was crucial. To this day, I use that poem as a touchstone and remembrance.

—Linda Swenson

10

GETTING USED TO YOUR NEW SOUND

Even after you have successfully developed your vocal instrument, a period of adjustment is almost always needed before you can actually use it in daily situations. This is awkward for everyone, and for some people it can be downright difficult.

For some lucky actors, of course, the period of adjustment is smooth and wonderful. Some people are able to allow their developed voices into both their lives and their acting quite easily, without any particular effort. This happens most often when the actor approves of the sound of his or her new vocal quality. "Strong" and "centered" are words I often hear.

But most people need to put some effort into actually using their newly developed voices all the time. Just because the voice is developed doesn't mean you will use it easily in every situation. Vocal habits are strong. Most of us have grown up using our voices in limited ways—using only a part of our vocal range.

I tell my students that, to be effective vocally when acting, they must use their voices fully and expressively *in daily life*.

There is a practical professional reason for saying this. You cannot say to a casting agent, "When I'm in front of the camera (or on the stage), my voice is quite different." The agent won't believe you.

More importantly, the way you use the voice in daily life is part of your professional image, part of the impression you make when you first meet a casting person or a director. In this country, we tend to typecast, and your voice is a large part of typecasting. When taking an interview, the actor must sound as if he or she can play the part. In fact, the interview is usually how an actor gets an audition in the first place.

When you meet casting people and other important figures in the business, your voice must also sound natural and honest. That can help you be recognizable as a potentially fine actor. If you produce your acting voice like a rabbit out of a hat, you will be seen as phony and hard to cast.

There are schools where the actor is taught to be very theatrical vocally—and word gets around. Many casting people in Los Angeles will not see actors from those programs, because they know the actors' voices will be too theatrical and, as a result, too impersonal and distancing for the film and television work being done there.

So as an actor, you must use your newly developed voice all the time—in your life as well as in your work. Full integration is the goal. That said, let me repeat that integrating your vocal changes into daily use does not happen instantly. Because you have strength in a particular muscle, or the ability to relax a particular muscle or express a certain emotional quality, does not mean that you will automatically do it. If you develop a good, strong voice—if you can hear it and feel it—then you often have to fight for your right to use it. You must make a conscious effort to integrate your new vocal changes into your life. You have to *decide* to do it, and then practice doing it. This is what integration involves.

INTEGRATING VOCAL CHANGES BY RELEASING TENSION

To integrate vocal changes into your life and work means, first, becoming aware of the sources of tension, and second, releasing the tension whenever it appears. There are four distinct types of tension, depending on the circumstances:

1. The physical tension you walk around with all the time. People have different habits, but the most common areas of physical tension involve the shoulders and abdomen. Some people hold their shoulders up or back, and their heads forward. Some tighten their bellies. Other people hunch their upper backs. And still others clench their teeth, or sit with their legs twisted around each other. We have all kinds of tension-producing habits that affect voice production.

2. Tension that occurs when you are speaking in front of a group. Sometimes the voice becomes tighter, or deeper, or higher, or more wobbly.

3. Tension while acting. Some people switch to a stagy voice. More often, nervousness creates tension that limits vocal production.

4. Finally, and most importantly, tension that arises in circumstances in which you are trying to express intense emotion. It can happen when you are having a fight in your offstage life or in the middle of your big scene onstage. The voice often becomes much higher in pitch or extremely tight. Often your voice comes out sounding like a squeak or a whine.

In each of these circumstances, you must become aware of what you are doing and what is happening in your body. As you do your daily vocal workout, you will learn more about your body and its influence on your voice. You will learn to release muscles governing vocal tension, which will then release the voice. Then, when you find yourself in the circumstances that alter the sound of your voice, you will be aware of what is happening in your body. Then, too, you will be able consciously to release the muscles causing vocal constraints. You will be able to accomplish this even when you are feeling very emotional or nervous.

DEALING WITH COMMON PROBLEMS

As an actor you must take responsibility for the condition of your instrument. It's not enough to say, "When I get emotional, my throat tightens up and my voice gets squeaky." Whatever happens to your voice when you get emotional is habit. You can change the involuntary reaction by developing your awareness and doing exercises on a regular basis.

As we've seen, it's usually not hard to figure out what is interfering with vocal production. Most problems can be traced to tension in the neck, jaw, and tongue, or to restricted breathing that disconnects the voice from the thought. Releasing specific parts of the body that govern the vocal instrument, and learning to connect breathing to the emotion you are feeling, will solve most of the problems.

If, at any given time, you experience a constrained vocal production, try to simply focus on these common limiting factors:

- Restricted breathing

- Lack of chest vibration

- Lack of sinus and nasal vibration

- Excessive neck tension

- Attempts to manipulate the voice when acting or speaking

If you find that you experience any of these problems in performance, review the complete exercises carefully, concentrating on the ones which focus directly on your problem.

And remember: You have to do the exercises on a daily basis. You have to understand what you are doing and why.

Finally, you really have to *want* your discoveries to work for you. This last is the key to success: Really fighting to integrate the vocal changes you make into your work. You have a right to your own voice.

It is necessary to explore the sensual aspects of the voice by teaching the actor to understand how the voice manifests itself in what he or she is feeling physically. Learning to let go of physical tension is paramount to a released breath. When this breath is released, the student can then begin to explore his or her own vocal power within the context of the given circumstances. As a result, the actor's voice and the physicality reflect his or her own emotional life. Good voice work is in the moment. It is fully informed by the breath, which expresses the actor's inner life and how the character relates to a situation.

—Thom Jones

11

CONNECTING YOUR VOICE TO YOUR EMOTIONAL LIFE

As I see it, a major point of voice training is to connect the voice to the actor's emotional life. Voice work is not "technical" work for the actor, for the voice is an intimate, natural part of what he or she is feeling and expressing. When the voice is released on the breath, there is a corresponding emotional release as well. If you have been doing the exercises with awareness of your emotions, you have taken the first very important step to accomplishing this.

This chapter provides you with three special exercises that should be approached after you have become familiar with the daily workout presented in Chapter 3. These exercises may feel very technical at first, but if you persevere, the results can be quite productive, and the exercises will show you how to be more honest.

Accordingly, the following exercises work best if the text you use has personal meaning for you.

1. Developing Vocal Directness

• Choose the first line of any speech from any scene, preferably one you are working on in a class or preparing for performance.

- Imagine that the sound you are going to make is coming from the belly. Make a **Huh** sound.

- Now, say the first word of your text, matching the pitch of the **Huh**. Remember, the image is that the sound is coming from your belly.

- After the first word, allow your voice to go anywhere it needs to go to express the remainder of the line.

- Repeat this procedure with each successive line of the speech. Start with **Huh**, and then match the first word of the line.

- Notice how starting each line with **Huh** puts your voice in a freer place.

- Practice this for twenty minutes a day for a few weeks. If you have success, then only *think* the **Huh** sound and match the first word.

- For most people, the sound will start in the lower half of the voice. This exercise is especially useful for women who tend to avoid the lower half of their voices.

- When first tapping any previously unused portion of your vocal tract, your voice may sound dull to you. However, anyone listening to you hears an impressive vocal and emotional feedback. Actors often say they feel "blank" when they first try this exercise. Using the voice in a new way usually feels wrong at first. However, it doesn't sound wrong.

- Continue to repeat and experiment with this exercise until it begins to feel comfortable.

The next two exercises are even more unusual in approach and have a startling impact when correctly executed. These exercises put you directly in touch with your feelings. You will discover what it feels like to actually *use* an emotionally connected voice.

2. Connecting Voice to Emotion:

- First, select a piece of material you like and feel connected to. It may be prose, poetry, or a speech from a play.

- Now begin the exercise: Close your eyes and ask yourself, "What am I feeling?" Often you are feeling many different things. You do not have to *label* the emotion(s) you feel, although you may. The important thing is to try to get in touch with whatever you are feeling, even if it seems wrong for this particular speech.

- Open your eyes and go to the text. Think the thoughts that are in the text and say the speech out loud—but try to stay in touch with your original feeling.

This may feel like tapping your head with one hand and rubbing your stomach with the other. Don't worry and don't be concerned about being appropriate or correct. This exercise allows you to be vocally open, even if what you are feeling is absurd for the text (by that, I mean it would be absurd to play a happy Hamlet or a joyful Medea). This feeling of being connected to your own emotions (and having an open instrument) can help you to be an honest actor. If you are open emotionally and instrumentally, and you are dealing with the thought "to be, or not to be," you will be affected emotionally and you will act genuinely.

Most actors doing this exercise are certain that the result could never be appropriate for actual performance. Others often say how believable and interesting the result is. What is happening is that several layers of emotion are being expressed, rather than one obvious feeling. This is what is going on with actors who find the results "interesting." If you are connected to what you are feeling, and if your voice is released, the thoughts from the text will influence your emotional life.

RECOGNIZING WHAT YOU ARE FEELING

Some actors have trouble with the beginning of Exercise 2, above, in which you are supposed to identify what you are feeling. Some say, "I can't tell what I'm feeling" or, "I feel nothing." An actor can't afford to be that unaware. If you cannot recognize, at least to some extent, what you are feeling at any given moment, you have to work to develop that ability. This is what I refer to as "getting in touch with your emotions"—being aware that you have feelings and having some sense of what they are. Usually, people trained from childhood not to express emotion have learned to block out feelings. But part of the actor's job is to express emotion, and if you are cut off from your own feelings, you will have to do some serious work on yourself.

Several good techniques can help you get in touch with your emotions, but I prefer the direct approach. If you are alive, you have emotions. I tell my students to ask themselves at least ten times throughout the day, "What am I feeling?" If you really do that, eventually you will have answers.

The answers do not have to be profound. You do not have to experience primal rage or joy. The answer can be many different things, simple or complex, trivial or substantial. Sometimes you can't label the feeling, but you can sense it.

The purpose of the technique is to learn to be open when you choose to be. You may have some resistance at first, but you can get in touch with yourself. I've seen it done many times.

3. Allowing Text to Influence Voice

- This exercise takes the previous exercise one step further.

- Sometimes an actor makes an intellectual choice concerning a character—the character is strong or weak, aggressive or shy.

The decision made, that doesn't mean an actor can skip making an emotional connection. But if your instrument is responsive, you can easily react emotionally and vocally to a thought.

- First, close your eyes. Release your belly. Breathe. Get in touch with your feeling, whatever it is.

- Think this thought: "Stop this right now!" Stay with that thought, and your emotions will change in some way.

- Now say the line out loud: "Stop this right now!" The new emotion will be expressed in your voice.

Students often say to me, "When I do this exercise, my voice doesn't come out the way I expected. It feels wrong. What should I do?" This is a good reaction, for the actor is really telling me that he or she has made an intellectual choice about interpretation but has left his emotional life and vocal instrument outside the process. The actor assumed that sometime later he (or she) would be able to bring in voice and emotion. But it won't work. The actor's performance will lack expression.

These are innovative and demanding exercises. They take real effort and concentration, but try them consistently and you will derive great results.

The way you breathe and the way you connect to your emotions have an impact on the moments of silence as well as the moments of speech.

—Francie Swift

12

BREATHING IS A PART OF YOUR ACTING

Breathing is that part of expression which you as an actor must deal with from the very beginning of your preparation. It cannot be added on at the end. Yet I have been told countless times by directors and acting teachers that actors have to get to the emotional essence of the role without being "distracted by vocal technicalities."

I agree that, when developing a role, actors should not be distracted by technicalities. But breathing is most definitely not a technicality. I always say to students that if you think breathing is "technical," try not breathing. We have to breathe to live.

I think confusion comes because actors often feel they are supposed to breathe in some kind of phony manner used only for acting, and they reject that. And I don't blame them. But it is breath that connects the actor to his or her emotion, and it is the voice which conveys that emotion to the audience. Observing the way a person is breathing is one of the ways we have of recognizing that individual's state of being. This automatically makes breathing a major component of the acting process.

For breathing to help you make the connection to emotional truth, it must be included from the beginning of your preparation—whether you are preparing a scene in class or rehearsing a play on Broadway. The last thing an actor needs is to go onstage or before the camera and be thinking about breathing as if it were a new piece of information.

Breathing is connected not only to your emotional state, but also to your desire or need to say something. Breathing is also tied to the meaning of the words. I sometimes see actors get up to work in class and take a big deep breath, usually while looking at the floor. Then they look at their partner. Then they start to talk. That big breath was connected to starting to act, rather than to what the actor wanted to express.

Understanding and opening up the breathing process—liberating the breath—allows the voice to reveal the character's inner emotional life. If you are breathing fully and if the breath is free, your voice will be personal and revealing.

LIBERATING THE BREATH

Human beings have found many bizarre ways to interfere with free and natural breathing. Breastplates and suits of armor, corsets and girdles, belts and high heels—all these limit the depth and freedom of the breath. They do this by physically limiting the movement of muscles that you use when breathing. For example, if the lower abdominal and transverse muscles are always pulled in, your breathing, and consequently your voice, cannot be responsive to your inner life. What's more, we have also devised many unnatural "breathing techniques." Some teach the actor to breathe the same way with each breath, eliminating any variety or freedom in the breathing. Since the actor is working hard to breathe uniformly, almost every sound becomes the same, regardless of the content of the words.

The truth is that an actor should breathe in response to the context of the situation, the meaning of the words, and the emotion being expressed. Ideally, the breath is free from external constraints and able to change freely all the time.

The basic secret of freeing the breath is this: If you release the lower abdominal muscles, the breath seems to go into your belly. (It doesn't, of course; in truth, it goes into your lungs.) Relaxing your abdomen, or belly, frees the diaphragm, the flat muscle that separates the abdomen from the chest cavity. In turn, your lungs are able to fill with as much air as you need. This is the natural way you breathe when you are sleeping.

If your abdominal muscles are released, the breath will automatically go into the lungs without effort. You don't need to push it there. Even if you need only a tiny amount of air, you still want to feel it start in the abdomen (rather than up in your chest). Likewise, if you need a lot of air in order to be very loud or express a long thought, the breath goes first to the belly and continues up into the expanding rib cage.

Let's do an exercise to clarify this point.

Take a very large breath and then say "Hi." Now, release the rest of the breath. This is a forced way to breathe; it feels quite unnatural. Obviously, you don't need all that breath just to say "Hi." If you simply release your abdominal muscles, you will automatically take in as much air as you need.

Let's do another quick exercise.

Imagine that you are out on the street and you see a friend about to walk in front of a moving truck. You want to shout "Stop!" Go ahead, shout it now.

If you called out "Stop!" in a way that will save your friend, I'm sure you didn't first say to yourself: "Large breath, now yell 'Stop!'" The point is you don't have to consciously think about how much air to take in. It's an automatic response. You will automatically take in the correct amount to express the thought—if you don't physically interfere with the natural process.

KNOWING WHERE TO BREATHE IN A SPEECH

Actors ask me where they should take a breath in a given speech. You can take a breath at any point the thought changes. (It's not usually a good idea to breathe according to punctuation.) If you are in touch with what you are saying and if you can keep your abdominal muscles relaxed, chances are your breathing will be perfect—that is, your breathing will become part of what you are expressing and also tell us something about the character.

INCREASING LUNG CAPACITY

Actors are often taught to speak a certain number of lines on one breath, so they will be able to sustain long speeches. This is an old voice-training idea, involving endless counting exercises to see how far you can get on one breath. Basically, what it produces is a big voice that can count.

Another ineffectual exercise is so-called "rib-reserved breathing," whereby an actor is taught to expand the rib cage and hold it that way, to provide some additional resonance. Unfortunately, this method creates great physical tension and separates the voice from inner emotional life and thought. The resulting voice tends to sound very announcer-like and devoid of emotion. This technique also creates a stiff, inexpressive body.

Still another method used to train actors to produce more sound is "punching" the abdominal muscles. In this exercise, the actor is usually asked to count or say **Huh** over and over again—the sound being forcibly pushed out with the muscles of the abdomen. But when you use muscle tension to push sound out, the voice cannot be emotionally revealing. Basically, this exercise connects the voice to the muscles rather than to the emotions. The sound you end up making is connected only to the violent muscular action.

Producing sound on the breath is the most expressive way to speak. Try these exercises now.

1. Take a breath, hold it in, and then say, "Hello, how are you?" Now let the breath out. The expression is on the sigh at the end of the sentence.

2. Take a breath, let it out, and now say, "Hello, how are you?" without taking another breath. The expression is on the sigh before you speak the words and thus the words themselves do not sound very expressive or honest, for there is no breath underneath them.

3. This time, do not breathe at all before you say, "Hello, how are you." There is no expression at all.

How, then, does an actor increase breath capacity? I suggest that you use actual lines from a scene and connect your speaking to an emotional and intellectual need to express the larger context of what you are saying. Don't leave your acting out of the process.

REDUCING NERVOUSNESS

For thousands of years actors have tried to come up with reliable techniques to reduce or eliminate nervousness at the beginning of a performance. One common method is to let out a long, slow, evenly controlled breath before the opening line. I call this *cooling out the breath*. Cooling out may be calming, but it dissipates emotions. When you "cool out," you are robbing yourself of your greatest gift: Your ability to express emotion.

However, there is a way to reduce nervousness, but still retain emotional content: Instead of cooling out, simply begin speaking your lines. You will feel more connected to the text, and soon your nervousness will subside.

BASIC RULES ON BREATHING

Breathing is very basic and natural, and I would simply impart these three basic rules for you to remember above all:

1. *Breathe through your mouth when you are speaking.* Breathing through your mouth is less contained and allows you to be more expressive. The breath goes to your lower abdomen first, and then up into the rib cage.

   Try this exercise:
   Say the line: "Hello, I'm glad to see you." Now take a very big breath through your nose and continue: "I'm glad I ran into you." Does it feel natural? Probably not.
   Now do the exercise again, but this time, breathe through your mouth. The phrase will be less held, much more natural, and more open.

2. *Free yourself up by letting go of physical tension and let the breath happen on its own.* Release the abdominal muscles and let the breath go there. (You don't need to manipulate your breath.)

3. *Take in only as much breath as you need to express the thought.* You want your breath to express your physical and emotional state. Little breaths for little thoughts, big breaths for big thoughts.

What is needed, more than anything, is a thorough understanding of why we take a breath (other than maintaining life—which is no small issue). Investigate this, observe it, and think about it. This assignment is not "technical," but fascinating when you really start to comprehend and explore something we all take for granted. So be an original—really think about this.

Most people would agree that it is impossible to tone the body by reading a book about exercise. Few would attempt to learn a spoken language by never speaking it. You must practice what you want to learn. Some days your practice will be a slog. On a special day, the practice will bring breakthroughs, like being struck by lightning. On all days, your practice will slowly and surely, through little steps of improvement, inescapably accumulate in your mastery of your instrument, your self. Experience precedes artistry. The doing comes first. Every day, do the work. There is never any good reason not to practice.

—Nels Hennum

13

PROFESSIONALISM

When I was in high school, I studied the trumpet. I had the good fortune to work with the first chair trumpeter of the Philadelphia Orchestra (under Eugene Ormandy). Although I never became a very good musician, I did learn what it was to be a professional. My teacher told me that the Philadelphia Orchestra had a tradition: If the group had a problem playing a certain section of music, they would play it one hundred times, very slowly. I learned from this man what it takes to deliver. It takes constant, sometimes demanding, work.

PHYSICAL ASPECTS OF VOICE TRAINING

I have never found it useful to use anatomical terms when working with actors on their voices. If one is interested in how the muscles of the body produce the voice, there is a great deal of information available, and it is quite easy to find. Knowing the physical workings of the voice does not automatically give you a good instrument, just as knowing anatomy does not make you a great dancer or athlete. I always tell students, if they want that knowledge—terrific, but the images used in the exercises work well.

Still, in general, it is important for your voice that you find a way to stay in good physical shape. After all, technically, the whole body is a resonator. Vocal cords make a very small sound, but it's your body which changes that small sound into what we recognize as the human voice. Consequently, if your body is toned and not held with too much muscle tension, you will produce the most voice with the smallest effort. It is too much effort that can make your voice less personal.

Everybody is different, and that is true about response to physical exercise as well. You alone can find the approach which works best for you. But if you are being asked to run across a stage, leap onto a platform, and give a big emotional speech, you must first contract the abdominals to make the leap, and then you must release the same abdominal muscles to produce the emotionally connected text. In other words, you have to be in good physical shape to stay in control of your voice. Physical stamina must be developed for you to be in the best condition vocally. Good voice work requires a basic understanding of how the entire physical instrument works.

ON THE NEED TO PRACTICE

After a month's study, a young actor once said to me, "You mean I have to do these vocal exercises again?" I was dumbfounded. Can you imagine a musician asking, "You mean I have to practice this scale again?"

The only way to develop your vocal instrument is through practice. Most people are born with potentially good vocal instruments, unless they have suffered some physiological damage. Over time, however, people develop bad physical and vocal habits that result in an inferior instrument. It takes regular practice to reverse the process. Discipline is thus absolutely necessary for results. You don't have to practice endlessly, but you do have to practice regularly and consistently.

Alarming though it may sound at first, I always tell my students that my approach to voice work is much like military training. In the armed forces, you learn to follow orders instantly. Basic training is total conditioning that prepares you to respond quickly and reliably— no questions, no hesitation, no negotiation—so that in a life-or-death encounter, when you are terrified, you can do your job effectively without pulling back or falling apart.

I am not suggesting that the actor's work is anything like a soldier's, but if you consider that an actor's professional life is full of pressure and intense, often intimidating moments—during interviews, auditions, screen tests, last-minute script changes, film shoots with millions of dollars riding on them, and opening nights—the comparison makes sense. A person has some physical tension even when lying down and reading a book, a comparatively relaxing activity. So imagine how tension increases when you are acting. Stress magnifies tension.

The actor's potential emotional reactions to stress range from simple nervousness and stage fright to sheer terror. Potential vocal reactions include high-pitched squeakiness, a dry and cracked sound, feeble voice production, severely restricted vocal range, and labored breathing. I've heard actors say they have nightmares in which they open their mouths to speak and no sound comes out.

If you practice releasing your voice daily, losing your voice is one thing you will probably never have to worry about. And when the stakes are raised in any situation, your vocal response will be immediate and full. This is partially due to your increased awareness. If you are conditioned properly, it is quite possible, for example, to feel nervous and still relax your neck and tongue. It is possible to be frightened out of your wits and tell yourself to breathe deeply, which allows you to feel connected to your emotions. But proper conditioning depends on daily, effective voice work. For something as important as your vocal instrument, ten to fifteen minutes a day is not much to ask.

Why daily? Like any other skill-related exercise, effective vocal work depends on consistency. Assuming that you are doing the right exercises in the right way, consistent practice is the most important part of voice training. After all, vocal development is all about changing habits. You are attempting to change *very strong, lifelong, physical habits of bodily tension.*

Tension affects different people differently. Some of us hold our shoulders up most of the time without realizing it. Some walk around with the tongue pressed against the roof of the mouth. Both habits interfere with the quality of the voice. As you develop new and better habits, your instrument will also develop. But in order to maintain those physical changes, you have to continue the exercises.

It's important to remember that, for a good while, what you are used to doing will feel better than what is new. New techniques require much reinforcement before they begin to feel comfortable the way old habits do.

Once you have improved your vocal fitness, you should be able to maintain it by exercising ten minutes each day.

LAPSES AND OTHER PROBLEMS

The vocal workout strengthens and stretches certain muscles, which makes them more responsive and gives them greater stamina. But the muscles responsible for producing sound react like any other muscles in your body: If you stop the exercises, the muscles soon return to their previous condition.

In the case of the vocal tract, you are working with relatively small and delicate muscle groups. On the positive side, that means it doesn't take long to bring about change. But it also means that you need to keep those muscles in shape. I have been doing voice exercises regularly for thirty-five years, and even now, when I take a vacation and stop doing those exercises, I can feel my voice tighten up and change in a matter of a few days. When this happens, friends often don't recognize my voice over the phone. More importantly, I lose the feeling of vocal strength. It takes me about a week to get back in shape after one of these brief interludes. Of course, the longer the lapse continues, the longer it takes to get your instrument back.

It seems to me that actors fail to make permanent vocal changes for two major reasons: Resistance to change and fear of losing control.

To be sure, change is not always comfortable and requires some effort. That's true for all of us. Resistance to change may look like lack of discipline or laziness, but it is simply part of human nature. But people who are truly ambitious always find some way to overcome their internal obstacles, at least to the extent that they can take that all-important first step. Getting started leads to a feeling of achievement, which generates an even greater commitment to change. This process is natural to all of us regardless of the type of change we are trying to make. Trust that once you begin, the beneficial results will motivate you to continue and build on your success.

A more serious problem than resistance is feeling that you are losing control. Actors always want to feel on top of their presentation of themselves. Voice work, however, is not about controlling the voice—it is about releasing the voice. I have heard actors say, "I don't want my voice to shake when I get emotional" or, "I feel too vulnerable and exposed when I let go." The fact is these responses are perfectly human. Voices do shake, and at times they do sound vulnerable. You can't have it both ways: To be open and honest vocally, and to be totally in control at the same time, are not possible.

Let's be realistic. There are times when you will not want to do the workouts. I certainly have these times. It is easy to put aside vocal conditioning if you have no auditions, rehearsals, or performances scheduled. However, it doesn't make sense to allow your voice to get out of shape. An actor needs to be prepared and in top form at all times, because he or she doesn't always know when an audition or an interview will come up. That having been said, what happens if you do take a day or a week off? Don't panic. Just get started again with the regular ten-minute-a-day workout.

I find these words from my wise friend and colleague Howard Stein highly motivating, not only about how one works best but also why one works:

> The crucial talent for the advancing of an actor's native talent is the talent to develop one's talent. In the days before professional training programs were established in the U.S.A., American

actors learned to develop their craft and skill with on-the-job-training. They developed into what were referred to as "real pros"—actors who could manage any situation with behavior that they had nurtured over their years on the stage, for the most part repeating what they had done onstage the last time. If one questioned a director (stage or film) about an actor's work on the set or on the stage by saying, "I've seen him (or her) do that hundreds of times already," the director (or producer) would answer, "That's what we bought! That actor is a real pro."

The appropriate and more productive way for an actor or actress to develop an original and imaginative talent is through training, listening, observing, and reading.

After forty years of teaching in theater training programs at the University of Iowa, Yale School of Drama, the University of Texas, the State University of New York at Purchase, and Columbia University, I can report with confidence that I have had significant contact with many, many, many students who were ambitious, but very, very, very few who were blessed with appetite. Those who were only ambitious were connected to the results of their profession: Money, fame, and celebrity. Those with appetite as well as ambition wanted to discover the challenges that their chosen profession placed before them and conquer those obstacles. They wanted to know the great roles. Why were those great roles greater than the less great roles? Those students loved their art, their profession, their profession's history, and the work necessary to nurture the skills and craft appropriate to their profession.

Know where you are; be honest and master the demands of your chosen field. If you want to be rich and famous more than anything else in the world, go for it with all your might, heart, and soul. If you want to master your art form, go for it with the same intensity!

My objective in life has been to develop an intelligent heart. Camus would call that instrument a compassionate mind. Bruno Bettelheim would call it an informed heart. Whatever the proper description, I yearned to cultivate a marriage between my heartfelt feelings and my energetic brain. Living a human life, I discovered early in my education, was a major task, necessitating concentration, diligence, discipline, and flexibility (an open mind!). I also discovered that the drama offered the clearest example (even the model) of the difficulty in living a valuable, successful, and fulfilling human life, precisely because the drama was based on the fundamental human condition of self-interest in conflict with the interest of another. I further learned, after my formal education, that the conflict begins the moment I get up in the morning and continues until I go off to bed, and not only off to bed, but until I go to sleep. That conflict is a never ending source of demand on anyone trying to live a good, human life. And the drama, for me, has been my best teacher.

AFTERWORD

I was lucky to grow up just outside of Philadelphia. In those days, all commercial productions first played out of town—usually in Philadelphia, Boston, and New Haven—before heading to Broadway. From the age of twelve, I was on that train to Philly and I saw every show I could, I was so hungry. Later, in college at Cornell, I kept up the practice. I managed to get to the opening in Rochester, New York, of Tennessee Williams' *Night of the Iguana*. It was a long trip, but worth it. I got to see Bette Davis and Margaret Leighton on the same stage in a Williams play. Inspiring.

Around the time that I was trekking to Rochester, I was also spending many hours in the wonderful Cornell library, where I discovered and read about great actors I had never heard of before. That was when I learned how important voice has always been to professional actors.

Although I had not yet thought about teaching voice, I started studying it with many teachers (Liz Dixon, Elizabeth Crawford, Lynn Masters, instructors in the Stanley Technique, various singing teachers—including Estelle Liebling) all before I worked intensely with Kristin Linklater. At this point in actor training (New York City in the 1960s), the voice was not emphasized and sometimes not even mentioned. If you wanted to study vocal production, you had to seek out a private teacher on your own.

In my experience, this served me well. So I encourage you to follow your interests and instincts in pursuing anything that has the potential to improve your acting. Look at dancers and musicians—they can be single-minded about their careers. Absorb everything you can about your chosen field. Go to the theater, see the best plays, read theater history, observe the finest actors in any medium. Think about and decide what is important for *you* to achieve.

I hope this book has been helpful. For me, the ideal result would be that you think differently about your voice than you did before you read it. As I said at the beginning, we tend to regard voice the way we regard a person's height—that it is what it is and cannot be changed. But this is not true. Your voice can always be developed and improved. Eventually you should become your own vocal coach. I always tell students, if in ten years you are doing something because I told you to, you need to rethink your work, because then something is wrong. You should own your vocal instrument. This is one more element of your craft that can be under your control. You will feel more on top of your talent and art, and be, indeed, more professional, when you yourself become responsible for making your voice heard.

SOURCES

There's a great deal of fascinating material available about voice training and acting, but you have to search for it. If you want to dig deeper into the subject, these sources will provide a start.

Acker, Barbara. "'I Charge Thee Speak': John Barrymore and His Voice Coach, Margaret Carrington." In *The Vocal Vision: Views on Voice by 24 Leading Teachers, Coaches and Directors*, ed. Marian Hampton and Barbara Acker. New York: Applause, 1997.

Barrymore, Lionel, and Cameron Shipp. *We Barrymores: As Told to Cameron Shipp*. New York: Appleton-Century-Crofts, 1951.

Behrman, S.N. "Do or Diaphragm." *The New Yorker*. May 25, 1935.

Berry, Cicely. *Voice and the Actor*. New York: Collier Books, 1973.

Brestoff, Richard, and Deborah Stevenson. *The Great Acting Teachers and Their Methods*. New Hampshire: Smith & Kraus, 1995.

Broun, Heywood "Mr. Shakespeare, Meet Mr. Tyson," February 1923, p. 33. Unidentified clipping in the Theatre Arts Collection. Harry Ransom Humanities Research Center, University of Texas, Austin.

Carrington, Margaret. "The John Barrymore I Knew." In *John Barrymore: A Bio-Bibliography*, by Martin F. Norden. Westport, CT: Greenwood Press, 1995.

Chen, Xiaomei. "A Stage in Search of a Tradition: The Dynamics of Form and Content in Post-Maoist Theatre." *Asian Theatre Journal*, Vol. 18, Number 2 (2001): 200–221.

Cole, Toby, and Helen Krich Chinoy. *Actors on Acting*. New York: Crown Publishing, 1974.

Collier, Constance (unpublished manuscript, Gene Fowler Collection. Boulder Libraries, University of Colorado).

Demastes, William W. *Beyond Naturalism: A New Realism in American Theatre*, Vol. 27. Westport, CT: Greenwood Press, 1988.

Edwards, Christine. *The Stanislavsky Heritage: Its Contribution to the Russian and American Theatre*. New York: New York University Press, 1965.

Fowler, Gene. *Good Night, Sweet Prince: The Life and Times of John Barrymore*. New York: Viking, 1943.

Gish, Lillian, and Ann Pinchot. *Lillian Gish: The Movies, Mr. Griffith, and Me*. Englewood Cliffs, NJ: Prentice Hall, 1969.

Grobel, Lawrence. *The Hustons: The Life and Times of a Hollywood Dynasty*. New York: Scribner's, 1989.

Hayes, Helen, and Katherine Hatch. *My Life in Three Acts*. New York: Harcourt Brace Jovanovich, 1990.

Hewitt, Barnard. *Theatre U.S.A., 1665–1957*. New York: McGraw-Hill Book Company, 1959.

Hopkins, Arthur. *To a Lonely Boy*. New York: The Book League of America, Inc., 1937.

——. *Reference Point; Reflections on Creative Ways in General with Special Reference to Creative Ways in Theatre*. New York: Samuel French, 1948.

Huston, John. *An Open Book*. New York: Knopf, 1980.

Ignatieva, Maria. *The Moscow Art Theatre's Stepdaughter: Stanislavsky and Olga Gzovskaya*. Theatre History Studies, 2002.

Kimbrough, Andrew McComb. "The Sound of Meaning: Theories of Voice in Twentieth-Century Thought and Performance." Ph.D. diss., Louisiana State University, 2002.

Kobler, John. *Damned in Paradise: The Life of John Barrymore.* New York: Atheneum, 1977.

Kristi, Grigori V. "The Training of an Actor in the Stanislavski School of Acting." In *Stanislavsky Today: Commentaries on K.S. Stanislavski,* edited and translated by Sonia Moore. New York: Center for Stanislavski Theatre Art, 1973.

Lesser, Wendy. *A Director Calls.* Berkeley: University of California Press, 1997.

Luce, William. *Barrymore.* New York: Samuel French, Inc., 1998.

Morrison, Michael A. *John Barrymore, Shakespearean Actor.* New York: Cambridge University Press, 1997.

Quinn, Anthony. *The Original Sin, a Self-Portrait.* Boston: Little Brown & Co., 1972.

Roach, Joseph R. *The Player's Passion: Studies in the Science of Acting.* Newark, DE: University of Delaware Press, 1985.

Rodenburg, Patsy. *The Right to Speak: Working with the Voice.* London: Methuen Drama, 1992.

Smith, Anna Deveare. "A Conversation with Peter Zeisler," *American Theatre,* July–August 1995.

Stebbins, Genevieve. *The Delsarte System of Dramatic Expression.* NY: Edgar S. Werner, 1886.

Steiner, Rudolf. *Speech and Drama*. Spring Valley, NY: Anthroposophic Press, 1986.

Strange, Michael. Michael Strange papers, 1917–1925. Billy Rose Theatre Collection. New York Public Library for the Performing Arts.

Taylor, J. Lark. "With Hey Ho!" (unpublished autobiography, University Archives, Vanderbilt University, Nashville, Tennessee).

Tuska, Jon. *Encounters with Filmmakers: Eight Career Studies, Vol. 29*. New York: Greenwood Publishing Co., 1991.

Weld, John. "September Song" (unpublished biography of Walter Huston, National Film Information Service, Academy Foundation, Center for Motion Picture Study, Beverly Hills, CA).

Young, Stark. "Terrible Storms of Pain," *New Republic*, December 1922. In *Theatre U.S.A., 1665–1957*, by Barnard Hewitt. New York: McGraw-Hill Book Company, 1959, p. 645.

INDEX